WORKTEXT
for

AUTOMOTIVE CHASSIS SYSTEMS

Third Edition

James D. Halderman
Sinclair Community College

Chase D. Mitchell
Utah Valley State College

Upper Saddle River, New Jersey
Columbus, Ohio

10 9 8 7 6 5 4 3 2 1

ISBN 0-13-048425-3

Preface

This worktext is designed to accompany the third edition of Automotive Chassis Systems. The activity sheets enclosed cover 100% of the NATEF task lists for ASE content areas A4 – Suspension and Steering, and A-5 – Brakes. Comprehensive appendixes include the following information.

Appendix 1 – Brakes (A5) NATEF Task List and Correlation Chart

This chart lists all of the NATEF tasks along with the page number of the activity sheet(s) that correlates to the tasks. This chart makes it easy for students and instructors to keep track of progress. The NATEF tasks are grouped according to priority to make it easier to concentrate on high-priority tasks.

Appendix 2 – Suspension and Steering (A4)

This chart lists all of the NATEF tasks along with the page number of the activity sheet(s) that correlates to the tasks. This chart makes it easy for students and instructors to keep track of progress. The NATEF tasks are grouped according to priority to make it easier to concentrate on high-priority tasks.

Chassis Systems Worktext Table of Contents

Page

Drum Brakes

Disc Brakes

Power Brake Units

Wheel Bearings and Miscellaneous Service

Page

Antilock Brake Systems (ABS)

General Suspension and Steering System Diagnosis

Steering System Diagnosis and Repair

Page

Suspension Systems Diagnosis and Repair

Wheel Alignment Diagnosis, Adjustment, and Repair

Material Safety Data Sheet (MSDS)

Meets NATEF Task: Environmental Safety Practices for Brakes (A5)

Name ________________________________ **Date** ______________________

Make/Model ____________________________ **Year** ________ **Instructor's OK** ☐

_____ **1.** Locate the MSDS sheets and describe their location______________________

____

_____ **2.** Select three commonly used chemicals or solvents. Record the following information from the MSDS:

- **Product name** ____

  chemical name(s) ____

  Does the chemical contain "chlor" or "fluor" which may indicate hazardous materials? **Yes** _____ **No** _____

  flash point = _________ (hopefully above 140° F)

  pH ________ (7 = neutral, higher than 7 = caustic (base), lower than 7 = acid)

- **Product name** ____

  chemical name(s) ____

  Does the chemical contain "chlor" or "fluor" which may indicate hazardous materials? **Yes** _____ **No** _____

  flash point = _________ (hopefully above 140° F)

  pH ________ (7 = neutral, higher than 7 = caustic (base), lower than 7 = acid)

- **Product name** ____

  chemical name(s) ____

  Does the chemical contain "chlor" or "fluor" which may indicate hazardous materials? **Yes** _____ **No** _____

  flash point = _________ (hopefully above 140° F)

  pH ________ (7 = neutral, higher than 7 = caustic (base), lower than 7 = acid)

Fire Extinguisher

Meets NATEF Task: Safety Requirement for Brakes (A5)

Name ______________________________ **Date** ______________________

Make/Model ___________________________ **Year** ________ **Instructor's OK** ☐

_____ **1.** Describe the location of the fire extinguishers in your building or shop and note the last inspection dates.

Type of Extinguisher	Location	Inspection Date
________________	________________	____________
________________	________________	____________
________________	________________	____________
________________	________________	____________

_____ **2.** Do any of the fire extinguishers need to be charged?

_____ Yes (which ones) ______________________________

_____ No

_____ **3.** Where can the fire extinguishers be recharged? List the name and telephone number of the company. ______________________________

_____ **4.** What is the cost to recharge the fire extinguishers?

a. Water = ______________

b. CO_2 = ______________

c. Dry chemical = ______________

Vehicle Hoisting

Meets NATEF Task: Safety Requirement for Brakes (A5)

Name ______________________________ **Date** ______________________

Make/Model __________________________ **Year** ________ **Instructor's OK** [ ]

Getting Ready to Hoist the Vehicle

_____ **1.** Drive the vehicle into position to be hoisted (lifted) being certain to center the vehicle in the stall.

_____ **2.** Pull the vehicle forward until the front tire rests on the tire pad (if equipped).

NOTE: Some long vehicles may have to be positioned forward of the pad and some short vehicles may have to be positioned behind the pad.

_____ **3.** Place the gear selector into the park position (if the vehicle has an automatic transmission/transaxle) or in neutral (if the vehicle has a manual transmission/transaxle) and firmly apply the parking brake.

_____ **4.** Lower the driver's side window before exiting the vehicle. (This step helps prevent keys from being accidentally being locked in the vehicle.)

_____ **5.** Position the arms and hoist pads under the frame or pinch weld areas of the body.

Hoisting the Vehicle

_____ **6.** Slowly raise the vehicle about one foot (30 cm) off the ground and check the stability of the vehicle by attempting to move the vehicle on the lift.

_____ **7.** If the vehicle is stable and all pads are properly positioned under the vehicle, continue hoisting the vehicle to the height needed.

NOTE: Best working conditions are at chest or elbow level.

_____ **8.** Be sure the safety latches have engaged before working under the vehicle.

Lowering the Vehicle

_____ **9.** To lower the vehicle, raise the hoist slightly, then release the safety latches.

_____ **10.** Lower the vehicle using the proper operating and safety release levers.

CAUTION: Do not look away while lowering the vehicle. One side of the vehicle could become stuck or something (or someone) could get under the vehicle.

_____ **11.** After lowering the hoist arms all the way to the floor, move the arms so that they will not be hit when the vehicle is driven out of the stall.

Safety Check

Meets NATEF Task: Safety Requirement for Brakes (A5)

Name ______________________________ **Date** ____________________

Make/Model ____________________________ **Year** ________ **Instructor's OK** [ ]

_____ **1.** Check the headlights (brights and dim).

_____ **2.** Check the taillights.

_____ **3.** Check the side marker lights.

_____ **4.** Check the license plate light.

_____ **5.** Check the brake lights.

_____ **6.** Check the turn signals.

_____ **7.** Check the back-up lights with the ignition switch "on" (engine "off") and the gear selector in reverse.

_____ **8.** Check the windshield wipers (all speeds) and wiper blades.

_____ **9.** Check the heater-defroster fan (all speeds).

_____ **10.** Check the condition of the tires (must have at least 2/32" of tread) and the tire pressure. Do not forget to check the spare tire!

_____ **11.** Check for looseness in the steering wheel (less than 2" of play).

_____ **12.** Check the 4-way emergency flashers.

_____ **13.** Check the horn.

_____ **14.** Listen for exhaust system leaks.

_____ **15.** Check the parking brake (maximum 8-10 "clicks" and should "hold" in drive).

VIN Code

Meets NATEF Task: (A5-A-3) Locate and Interpret Vehicle Identification Numbers (P-1)

Name ______________________________ **Date** ______________________

Make/Model ________________________ **Year** ________ **Instructor's OK** [ ]

VIN Number ____________________________

- The first number or letter designates the **country of origin** = ____________

1 = United States	9 = Brazil	V = France
2 = Canada	J = Japan	W = Germany
3 = Mexico	K = Korea	Y = Sweden
4 = United States	L = Taiwan	Z = Italy
6 = Australia	S = England	

- The model of the vehicle is commonly the fourth or fifth character. **Model?** _______
- The eighth character is often the engine code. (Some engines cannot be determined by the VIN number.) **Engine code:** ________________
- The tenth character represents the year on all vehicles. See the following chart.

Vin Year Chart **Year?** ______________

A = 1980	L = 1990	Y = 2000
B = 1981	M = 1991	1 = 2001
C = 1982	N = 1992	2 = 2002
D = 1983	P = 1993	3 = 2003
E = 1984	R = 1994	4 = 2004
F = 1985	S = 1995	5 = 2005
G = 1986	T = 1996	6 = 2006
H = 1987	V = 1997	7 = 2007
J = 1988	W = 1998	8 = 2008
K = 1989	X = 1999	9 = 2009

Vehicle Brake System Information

Meets NATEF Task: (A5-A-2) Research Vehicle Service Information (P-1)

Name ______________________________ **Date** ______________________

Make/Model ________________________ **Year** ________ **Instructor's OK** [ ]

Consult vehicle manufacturer's service information to determine the following:

_____ **1.** Brake related technical service bulletins (TSBs):

A. Topic ____________________ Bulletin Number ____________________

Problem/Correction: ____

B. Topic ____________________ Bulletin Number ____________________

Problem/Correction: ____

_____ **2.** Front brake service information:

A. Minimum thickness of front disc brake pads: ______________

B. Minimum thickness of front disc brake rotor: ______________

_____ **3.** Rear brake service information:

A. Minimum thickness of rear friction material: ______________

B. Maximum allowable drum or minimum allowable rear disc brake rotor thickness: ______________

_____ **4.** ABS/hydraulic service information:

A. Brand and type of ABS: ________________________________

B. Bleeding procedure: __________, __________, __________, __________

C. Wheel speed sensor resistance/gap: Front = _______ Rear = _______

_____ **5.** Research the vehicle's service history and record all brake system-related previous service or repairs.

____

____

____

____

Base Brake Identification

Meets NATEF Task: (A5-A-2) Research Applicable Vehicle and Service Information (P-1)

Name ________________________________ **Date** ______________________

Make/Model ________________________ **Year** ________ **Instructor's OK** [ ]

_____ **1.** The vehicle being inspected is equipped with what type of base brakes?

_____ Four-wheel drum brakes (old vehicles)

_____ Four-wheel disc brakes

_____ Front disc brakes/rear drum brakes

_____ Other (describe) ____________________

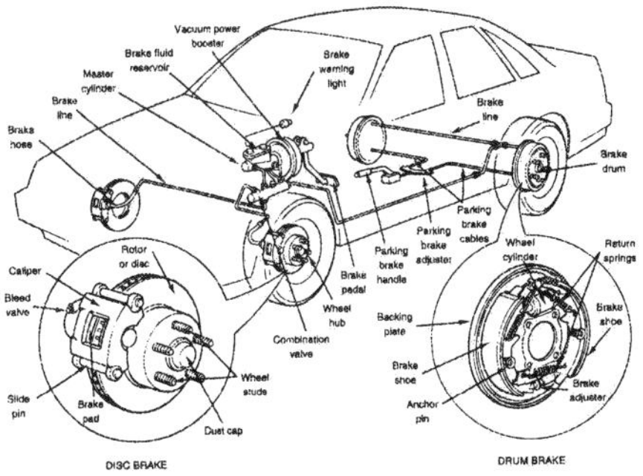

_____ **2.** Is the vehicle equipped with an antilock braking system? _____ Yes _____ No

If yes, describe the type of system ________________________________

_____ **3.** Consult the vehicle manufacturer's service information and determine the specified brake fluid:

_____ DOT 3

_____ DOT 4

_____ DOT 5.1

_____ DOT 5.0

_____ Other (specify) ________________________________

_____ **4.** Check the condition of the brake fluid.

_____ Clear (like new)

_____ Amber

_____ Dark amber

_____ Black

_____ Other (describe) ________________________________

Identify and Interpret Brake Concerns

Meets NATEF Task: (A5-A-1) Identify and Interpret Brake System Concern and Determine Necessary Action (P-1)

Name ______________________________ **Date** ______________________

Make/Model ___________________________ **Year** ________ **Instructor's OK** [ ]

_____ **1.** Verify the customer's concern regarding brake system performance and identify areas of concern (check all that apply).

_____ Red brake warning light on
_____ Amber ABS warning light on
_____ Noise during braking
_____ Noise while driving
_____ Pulling during braking
_____ Hard brake pedal
_____ Low brake pedal
_____ Spongy brake pedal
_____ Pulsating brake pedal
_____ Steering wheel vibration during breaking
_____ Hard to stop
_____ Parking brake will not hold the vehicle
_____ ABS activates at low speed
_____ Unusual noise
_____ Unusual smell
_____ Other (describe)
____

_____ **2.** Perform a thorough visual inspection and note any possible problems.

_____ Tires (all the same brand, size, inflation, and condition)
_____ **OK** _____ **NOT OK** **Describe** ______________________

_____ Brake fluid (check all that apply)
_____ **OK** _____ **Dirty** _____ **Low**

_____ Front disc brakes
_____ **OK** _____ **NOT OK** **Describe** ______________________

_____ Rear brakes
_____ **OK** _____ **NOT OK** **Describe** ______________________

_____ Hydraulic lines, parts, and fittings
_____ **OK** _____ **NOT OK** **Describe** ______________________

_____ **3.** Based on the symptoms and the inspection, what service and/or parts will be needed to restore like-new braking system performance?

____

____

Red Brake Warning Lamp Diagnosis

Meets NATEF Task: (A5-B-11) Inspect, Test and/or Replace Components of Brake Warning Light System (P-3)

Name ________________________________ **Date** ________________________

Make/Model ____________________________ **Year** ________ **Instructor's OK** ☐

_____ **1.** Does the vehicle use a brake fluid level sensor?

___ **Yes** ___ **No**

(If yes, describe the location: ________________________________.)

_____ **2.** Does the vehicle use a pressure differential switch?

___ **Yes** ___ **No**

(If yes, describe the location: ________________________________.)

_____ **3.** With the ignition key on, engine off (KOEO), apply the parking brake. Did the red brake warning lamp light?

___ **Yes** ___ **No**

(If no, why not? ________________________________)

_____ **4.** Unplug the wiring connector from the brake fluid level sensor or pressure differential switch. With the key on, engine off (KOEO), did the red brake warning lamp light?

___ **Yes** ___ **No** (It should not have come on.)

_____ **5.** State the vehicle manufacturer's recommended inspection, testing, and replacement procedures:

____

____

____

____

Brake Pedal Height

Meet NATEF Task: (A5-B-2) Measure Brake Pedal Height; Determine Necessary Action (P-2)

Name ______________________________ **Date** ______________________

Make/Model ___________________________ **Year** ________ **Instructor's OK** ☐

_____ **1.** State the vehicle manufacturer's specified brake height testing procedure:

____

____

____

_____ **2.** Measure the brake pedal height from the bottom of the steering wheel to the brake pedal.

________ = inch (cm)

_____ **3.** Depress the brake pedal until the brakes are applied and measure the brake pedal height.

________ = inch (cm)

_____ **4.** Subtract the second reading from the first reading. This is the brake pedal travel.

_______ = brake pedal travel (should be a maximum of 2.0 to 2.5 in.)

_____ **5.** List three items that could cause a greater than normal brake pedal travel.

A. ______________________________

B. ______________________________

C. ______________________________

Bench Bleeding the Master Cylinder

Meet NATEF Task: (A5-B-4) Bench Bleed Master Cylinder (P-1)

Name ________________________ **Date** ____________________

Make/Model ____________________ **Year** ________ **Instructor's OK** ☐

Before a replacement master cylinder is installed in a vehicle, most vehicle manufacturers recommend that the master cylinder be bled.

_____ **1.** Clamp the ears of the master cylinder in a suitable vise.

> **CAUTION:** Do not clamp the body of the master cylinder or bore distortion can occur.

_____ **2.** Install tubes into the outlets of the master cylinder and direct the tubes near the top of the open reservoir.

_____ **3.** Fill the master cylinder reservoir with clean DOT 3 brake fluid from a sealed container.

_____ **4.** Using a blunt tool, such as a rounded dowel rod or a Phillips screwdriver, slowly stroke the master cylinder.

_____ **5.** Continue stroking the master cylinder until a solid stream of brake fluid is observed flowing out of the tubes and into the reservoir.

_____ **6.** Remove the bleeding tubes and unclamp the master cylinder. The master cylinder can now be installed on the vehicle where additional bleeding at the outlet fitting may be necessary.

Master Cylinder Operation Testing

Meet NATEF Task: (A5-B-3) Check Master Cylinder for External and Internal Leaks and Proper Operation (P-2)

Name ______________________________ **Date** ____________________

Make/Model ________________________ **Year** ________ **Instructor's OK** [ ]

_____ **1.** Check visually for signs of external brake fluid leaks.

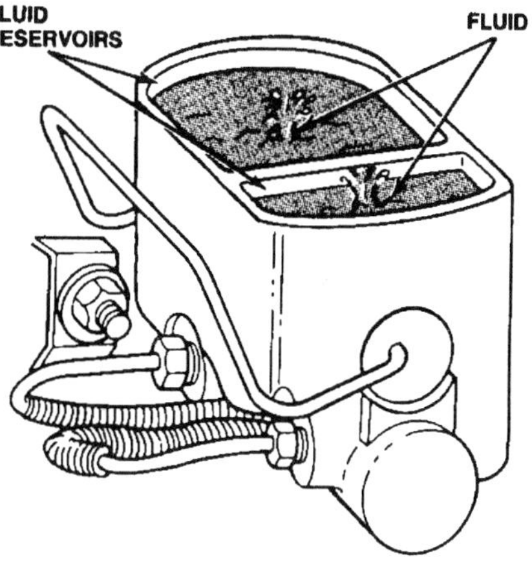

_____ **OK** _____ **NOT OK**

Describe location ____________________

FLUID RESERVOIRS

FLUID

_____ **2.** Check for internal leakage by observing the level of brake fluid in the front compared to the rear.

A. Is the level higher in the front than the rear? ____ **Yes** ____ **No**

B. Is the brake pedal lower than normal? ____ **Yes** ____ **No**

If yes to both A and B above, then the master cylinder is leaking internally and must be replaced.

_____ **3.** Have an assistant depress the brake pedal while watching the brake fluid in the master cylinder reservoir. The brake fluid should be seen to move as the brake pedal is being depressed if the sealing caps are OK and positioned correctly.

Movement observed? ____ **Yes** ____ **No**

If brake fluid does not move and there is a breaking system problem, the master cylinder or linkage adjustment is faulty.

Hydraulic Pressure Analysis

Meet NATEF Task: (A5-B-1) Diagnose Pressure Concerns in the Brake System Using Hydraulic Principles (P-1)

Name ______________________________ **Date** ______________________

Make/Model __________________________ **Year** _______ **Instructor's OK** ☐

_____ **1.** Remove the disc brake calipers and install a force gauge between the caliper piston and the caliper housing.

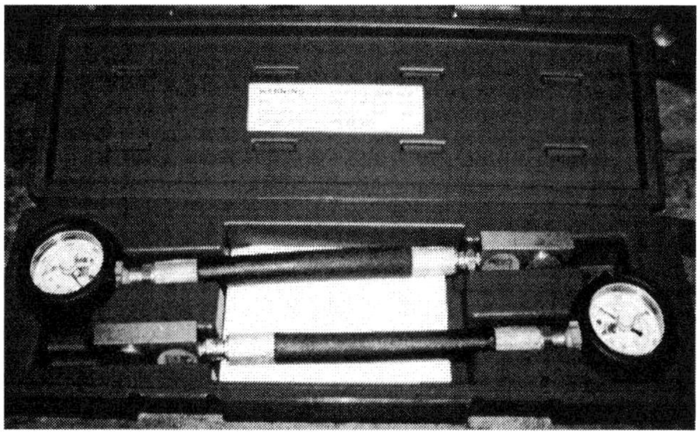

_____ **2.** Depress the brake pedal and observe the force readings.

Left side = ______ pounds Right side = ______ pounds

The readings should be the same. **OK** _____ **NOT OK** _____

_____ **3.** List possible causes that could prevent the force reading to be different from one side to the other.

A. ____

B. ____

C. ____

Hydraulic System Fault Analysis

Meet NATEF Task: (A5-B-5) Diagnose Braking Concerns Caused by Hydraulic Malfunctions (P-1)

Name ______________________________ **Date** ______________________

Make/Model __________________________ **Year** ________ **Instructor's OK** ☐

Poor stopping or dragging brakes or pulling can be caused by hydraulic system failure or faults.

_____ **1.** Verify proper operation of the base brakes.

_____ OK
_____ Pulls to the left during braking (see Step #2).
_____ Pulls to the right during braking (see Step #2).
_____ Brakes do not release fully (see Step #3).
_____ Poor stopping (see Step #4).
_____ Other brake system concerns (describe) ______________________

_____ **2.** Pulling can be caused by a stuck caliper piston on the side *opposite* the direction of the pull.

If there is a pull to the right during braking, check the left side caliper.
OK ____ **NOT OK** ____

If there is a pull to the left during braking, check the right side caliper.
OK ____ **NOT OK** ____

_____ **3.** Brakes that do not fully release can be caused by a fault with the flexible brake hose and/or a stuck caliper piston

Visually check the flexible brake hose. **OK** ____ **NOT OK** ____

Check that the caliper piston can be moved into the caliper bore easily.
OK ____ **NOT OK** ____

_____ **4.** Poor stopping can be caused by a stuck caliper or wheel cylinder piston. Check that all hydraulic pistons are free.

LF = **OK** ____ **NOT OK** ____
RF = **OK** ____ **NOT OK** ____
LR = **OK** ____ **NOT OK** ____
RR= **OK** ____ **NOT OK** ____

Brake Hose and Line Inspection

Meet NATEF Task: (A5-B-6) Inspect Brake Lines and Flexible Hose for Faults and Determine Necessary Action (P-2)

Name ______________________________ **Date** ______________________

Make/Model ______________________ **Year** ________ **Instructor's OK** ☐

_____ **1.** Hoist the vehicle safely.

_____ **2.** Remove all four wheels.

_____ **3.** Carefully inspect the flexible brake hoses on the left front, right front, and rear (one or two flexible hoses) for the following:

_____ Leaks **OK** ___ **NOT OK** ___ Which hose(s)? ________________

_____ Kinks **OK** ___ **NOT OK** ___ Which hose(s)? ________________

_____ Cracks **OK** ___ **NOT OK** ___ Which hose(s)? ________________

_____ Bulges or wear **OK** ___ **NOT OK** ___ Which hose(s)? ___________

_____ **4.** Carefully inspect the steel brake lines from the master cylinder to the junction with the flexible brake lines and check for the following:

_____ Leaks **OK** ___ **NOT OK** ___ Fault location? ________________

_____ Dents **OK** ___ **NOT OK** ___ Fault location? ________________

_____ Loose fittings or supports **OK** ___ **NOT OK** ___

Fault location? ________________

_____ **5.** What corrective action is necessary to return the brake line and hoses to proper condition?

____

____

Brake Line Flaring

Meet NATEF Task: (A5-B-7) Fabricate and/or Install Brake Line (Double Flare and ISO Types) (P-2)

Name ______________________________ **Date** ______________________

Make/Model ___________________________ **Year** ________ **Instructor's OK** ☐

_____ **1.** Consult the vehicle manufacturer's service information and select the specified diameter of steel brake line. Which size outside diameter (O.D.) is needed for the application?

_____ 3/16" (4.8 mm)

_____ 1/4" (6.4 mm)

_____ 5/16" (7.9 mm)

A B

FIRST STEP FINISHED DOUBLE FLARE

_____ **2.** Using a tubing bender, bend the sample line with a right angle (90°) bend.

Instructor's OK ______________________

_____ **3.** Using the proper tool, perform a double flare on one end of the brake line.

Instructor's OK ______________________

_____ **4.** Using the proper tool, perform an ISO flare on the other end of the brake line.

Instructor's OK ______________________

Brake Fluid

Meet NATEF Task: (A5-B-8) Brake Fluid Handling, Storage, and Filling (P-1)

Name ______________________________ **Date** ______________________

Make/Model ________________________ **Year** ________ **Instructor's OK** [ ]

_____ **1.** Consult the vehicle manufacturer's service information and determine the specified type of brake fluid.

____ DOT 3 ____ DOT 4 ____ Other (specify) ____________________

_____ **2.** All brake fluid should be stored in a sealed container. Specify what type and size container of container is being used.

_____ Metal (preferred because air cannot penetrate metal)

_____ Plastic (makes shelf life shorter because air can penetrate most plastic)

_____ Size (number of ounces or ml) ____________

_____ **3.** Brake fluid can remove paint so protective covers should be used whenever handling brake fluid. Check all that should be done when handling brake fluid.

_____ Use fender covers

_____ Wear protective gloves

_____ **4.** Fill brake fluid to the "MAX" line on the master cylinder reservoir.

CAUTION: If the brake fluid level is too high, the brakes may self-apply when the normal operation of the wheel brakes warms the brake fluid, which expands in volume. If the brake fluid is unable to expand in the master cylinder reservoir, the pressure increases and the brakes can be applied even though the driver did not depress the brake pedal.

Metering Valve Inspection and Testing

Meet NATEF Task: (A5-B-9) Inspect, Test, and/or Replace Metering (Hold-Off) Valve (P-2)

Name ______________________________ **Date** ______________________

Make/Model __________________________ **Year** ________ **Instructor's OK** ☐

A defective metering valve can leak brake fluid and/or cause the front brakes to apply before the rear brakes. This is most commonly noticed on slippery surfaces such as on snow or ice or on rain-slick roads. If the front brakes lock up during these conditions, the front wheels cannot be steered. Inspect the metering for these two conditions:

_____ **1.** Leakage - Look at the bottom on the metering valve for brake fluid leakage. (Ignore slight dampness.) Replace the metering valve assembly if leaking.

_____ **2.** As the pressure builds to the front brakes, the metering valve stem should move. If it does not, replace the valve.

_____ **3.** State the vehicle manufacturer's service information for the recommended metering valve testing procedure:

____

____

____

_____ **4.** More accurate testing of the metering valve can be accomplished using pressure gauges. Install two gauges, one in the pressure line coming from the master cylinder and the other in the outlet line leading to the front brakes.

_____ **5.** Depress the brake pedal. Both gauges should read the same until about 3-30 psi (20 to 200 kPa) when the metering valve shuts thereby delaying the operation of the front brakes.

_____ **6.** The master cylinder outlet gauge should show an increase in pressure as the brake pedal is depressed further.

_____ **7.** Once 75 to 300 psi is reached, the gauge showing pressure to the front brakes should match the pressure from the master cylinder. If the pressures do not match these ranges, the metering valve assembly should be replaced.

HINT: Neither the metering valve nor the proportioning valve can cause a pull to one side if defective. The metering valve controls *both* front brakes, and the proportioning valve controls *both* rear brakes. A defective master cylinder cannot cause a pull either. Therefore, if a vehicle pulls to one side during a stop, look for problems in the individual wheel brakes, hoses or suspension.

Proportioning Valve Inspection and Testing

Meet NATEF Task: (A5-B-9) Inspect, Test, and/or Replace Proportioning Valve (P-2)

Name ______________________________ **Date** ______________________

Make/Model ___________________________ **Year** ________ **Instructor's OK** ☐

A defective proportioning valve usually allows rear brake pressure to increase too rapidly, causing the rear wheels to lock up during hard braking. If the proportioning valve is height sensing, verify proper vehicle ride (trim) height and adjustment of the operating lever.

Always follow the exact testing procedure specified by the vehicle manufacturer.

_____ **1.** Install one gauge into the brake line from the master cylinder and the second gauge to the rear brake outlet of the proportioning valve.

_____ **2.** While an assistant depresses the brake pedal, observe the two gauges. Both gauges should register an increasing pressure as the brake pedal is depressed until the split point.

_____ **3.** After the split point, the gauge connected to the proportioning valve (rear brakes) should increase at a slower rate than the reading on the gauge connected to the master cylinder.

OK _____ **NOT OK** _____

If the pressures do not react as described, the proportioning valve should be *replaced.*

NOTE: The same procedure can be performed on a diagonal split-type system as used on most front-wheel-drive vehicles.

_____ **4.** State the vehicle manufacturer's recommended inspection, testing, and replacement procedure:

____

____

____

____

Pressure Differential Switch Inspection

Meet NATEF Task: (A5-B-9) Inspect, Test, and/or Replace Pressure Differential Switch (P-2)

Name ______________________________ **Date** ____________________

Make/Model ________________________ **Year** ________ **Instructor's OK** ☐

_____ **1.** A pressure-differential switch is used on all vehicles built after 1967 with dual master cylinders to warn the driver of a loss of pressure in one of the two separate systems by lighting the dashboard red brake warning indicator lamp.

_____ **2.** The brake lines from both the front and the rear sections of the master cylinder are sent to this switch which lights the brake warning indicator lamp in the event of a "difference in pressure" between the two sections.

_____ **3.** A failure in one part of the brake system does not result in a failure of the entire hydraulic system. After the hydraulic system has been repaired and bled, moderate pressure on the brake pedal will center the piston in the switch and turn off the warning lamp.

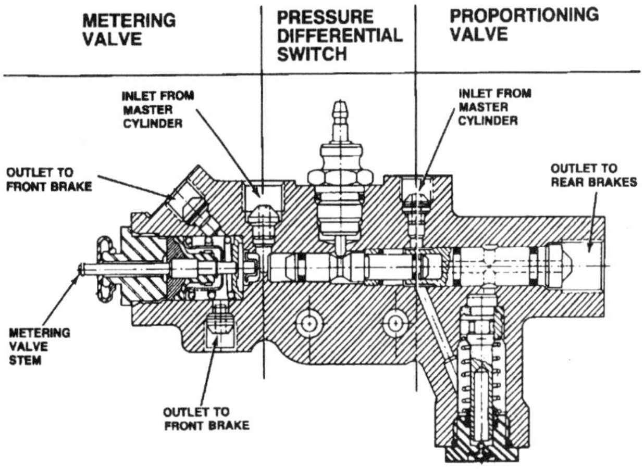

_____ **4.** If the lamp remains on, it may be necessary to:

A. Apply light pressure to the brake pedal.
B. Momentarily open the bleeder valve on the side that did not have the failure.

This procedure should center the pressure differential switch valve in those vehicles not equipped with self-centering springs.

_____ **5.** State the vehicle manufacturer's recommended inspection, testing, and replacement procedures:

____

____

____

____

Height-Sensing Proportioning Valve

Meet NATEF Task: (A5-B-10) Inspect, Test, and Adjust Height Sensing Proportioning Valve (P-3)

Name ______________________________ **Date** ______________________

Make/Model ________________________ **Year** ________ **Instructor's OK** ☐

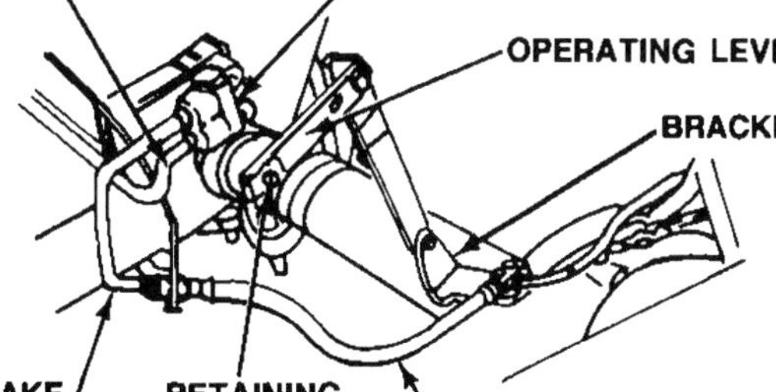

_____ **1.** Describe the location of the height-sensing proportioning valve.

____

____

____

_____ **2.** Visually check for leakage at the valve or damage to the linkage between the valve and the rear suspension.

OK ____ **NOT OK** ____ Describe fault: ______________________

_____ **3.** List the steps specified by the service information regarding how the valves or linkage should be adjusted:

____

____

____

____

Manual Brake Bleeding

Meets NATEF Task: (A5-B-12) Bleed the Brake System (P-1)

Name ______________________________ **Date** ______________________

Make/Model ____________________________ **Year** ________ **Instructor's OK** [ ]

_____ **1.** Check the service information for the specified brake bleeding procedure for the vehicle being serviced.

_____ **2.** Fill the master cylinder reservoir with clean brake fluid from a sealed container.

_____ **3.** Hoist the vehicle safely.

_____ **4.** Open the right rear bleeder valve and have an assistant slowly depress the brake pedal to bleed the wheel cylinder/caliper. Close the bleeder valve and have the assistant slowly release force on the brake pedal. Wait 15 seconds and repeat the process until a solid stream of brake fluid is observed.

_____ **5.** Repeat the bleeding procedures for the left-rear, right-front, and then the left-front wheel brakes.

_____ **6.** After all four wheel brakes have been bled, lower the vehicle and fill the master cylinder to the full mark.

> **CAUTION:** Check the master cylinder reservoir frequently and refill as necessary with clean brake fluid. Do not overfill a master cylinder reservoir.

_____ **7.** Test drive the vehicle checking for proper brake operation before returning the vehicle to the customer.

Pressure Brake Bleeding

Meets NATEF Task: (A5-B-12) Bleed the Brake System (P-1)

Name ______________________________ **Date** ______________________

Make/Model __________________________ **Year** ________ **Instructor's OK** ☐

_____ **1.** Check the service information for the specified brake bleeding procedure for the vehicle being serviced.

_____ **2.** Fill the master cylinder reservoir with clean brake fluid from a sealed container.

_____ **3.** Hoist the vehicle safely.

_____ **4.** Open the right rear bleeder valve and use a pressure bleeder attached to the master cylinder using the correct adapter(s) to bleed the wheel cylinder/caliper until a solid stream of brake fluid is observed.

_____ **5.** Repeat the bleeding procedures for the left-rear, right-front, and then the left-front wheel brakes.

_____ **6.** After all four wheel brakes have been bled, lower the vehicle and fill the master cylinder to the full mark.

> **CAUTION:** Check the master cylinder reservoir frequently and refill as necessary with clean brake fluid. Do not overfill a master cylinder reservoir.

_____ **7.** Test drive the vehicle checking for proper brake operation before returning the vehicle to the customer.

Vacuum Brake Bleeding

Meets NATEF Task: (A5-B-12) Bleed the Brake System (P-1)

Name ______________________ **Date** ______________

Make/Model ____________________ **Year** ________ **Instructor's OK** ☐

_____ **1.** Check the service information for the specified brake bleeding procedure for the vehicle being serviced.

_____ **2.** Fill the master cylinder reservoir with clean brake fluid from a sealed container.

_____ **3.** Hoist the vehicle safely.

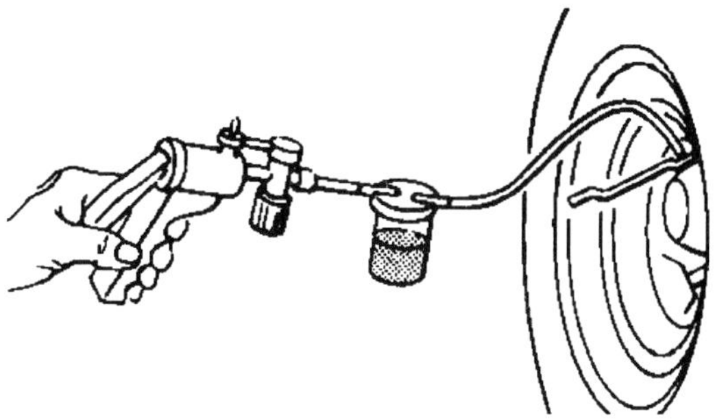

_____ **4.** Open the right rear bleeder valve and use a hand-operated or air-operated vacuum bleeder to bleed the wheel cylinder/caliper until a solid stream of brake fluid is observed.

_____ **5.** Repeat the bleeding procedures for the left-rear, right-front, and then the left-front wheel brakes.

_____ **6.** After all four wheel brakes have been bled, lower the vehicle and fill the master cylinder to the full mark.

> **CAUTION:** Check the master cylinder reservoir frequently and refill as necessary with clean brake fluid. Do not overfill a master cylinder reservoir.

_____ **7.** Test drive the vehicle checking for proper brake operation before returning the vehicle to the customer.

Gravity Brake Bleeding

Meets NATEF Task: (A5-B-12) Bleed the Brake System (P-1)

Name ______________________ **Date** ______________________

Make/Model ______________________ **Year** ________ **Instructor's OK** ☐

_____ **1.** Check the service information for the specified brake bleeding procedure for the vehicle being serviced.

_____ **2.** Fill the master cylinder reservoir with clean brake fluid from a sealed container.

_____ **3.** Hoist the vehicle safely.

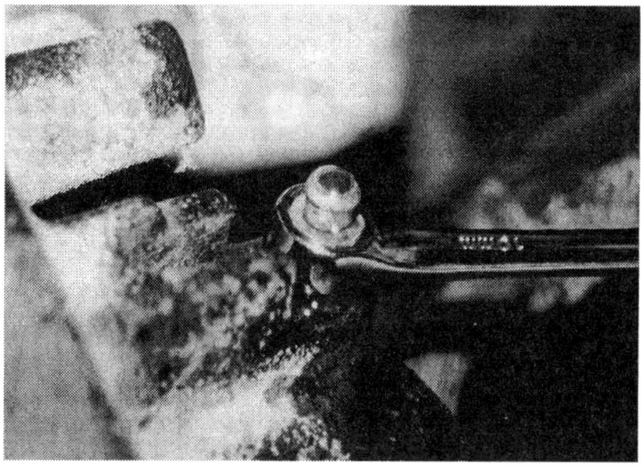

_____ **4.** Open the right rear bleeder valve and wait until about a drip-per-second of brake fluid is observed coming out of the bleeder valve and close the bleeder valve.

_____ **5.** Repeat the bleeding procedures for the left-rear, right-front, and then the left-front wheel brakes.

_____ **6.** After all four wheel brakes have been bled, lower the vehicle and fill the master cylinder to the full mark.

CAUTION: Check the master cylinder reservoir frequently and refill as necessary with clean brake fluid. Do not overfill a master cylinder reservoir.

_____ **7.** Test drive the vehicle checking for proper brake operation before returning the vehicle to the customer.

Surge Brake Bleeding

Meets NATEF Task: (A5-B-12) Bleed the Brake System (P-1)

Name ______________________________ **Date** ______________________

Make/Model ________________________ **Year** ________ **Instructor's OK** ☐

_____ **1.** Check the service information for the specified brake bleeding procedure for the vehicle being serviced.

_____ **2.** Slip the plastic hose over the bleeder screw of the wheel cylinder or caliper to be bled and submerge the end of the tube in the jar of brake fluid.

_____ **3.** Open the bleeder screw approximately one-half turn.

_____ **4.** With the bleeder screw *open*, have your assistant rapidly pump the brake pedal several times. Air bubbles should come out with the brake fluid.

_____ **5.** While your assistant holds the brake pedal to the floor, close the bleeder screw.

_____ **6.** Repeat steps 2 through 4 at each bleeder screw in the recommended order.

_____ **7.** Re-bleed the system using one of the four other methods described above.

Brake Fluid Flush and Fill

Meets NATEF Task: (A5-B-13) Flush Hydraulic System (P-3)

Name ______________________________ **Date** ____________________

Make/Model ____________________________ **Year** ________ **Instructor's OK** ☐

Many vehicle manufacturers recommend the replacement of brake fluid every 2 or 3 years (24,000 - 36,000 miles or 38,000 - 58,000 km).

_____ **1.** Check the service information for the specified brake bleeding procedure for the vehicle being serviced.

_____ **2.** Use a turkey baster or similar tool to remove most of the old brake fluid from the master cylinder reservoir.

_____ **3.** Refill the master cylinder with new brake fluid from a sealed container.

_____ **4.** Hoist the vehicle safely.

_____ **5.** Bleed the brake fluid from the right rear wheel brake until clean brake fluid is observed.

_____ **6.** Repeat the bleeding process for the left rear, right front, then the left front wheel brakes.

> **NOTE:** Check the level of the brake fluid often and refill as necessary. Do not allow the master cylinder reservoir to become empty.

_____ **7.** After all the wheel brakes have been bled with clean brake fluid, lower the vehicle and test drive checking for proper operation of the brakes before returning the vehicle to the customer.

Drum Brake Problem Diagnosis

Meets NATEF Task: (A5-C-1) Diagnose Drum Brake Concerns and Determine Necessary Action (P-1)

Name ______________________ **Date** ______________

Make/Model ____________________ **Year** ________ **Instructor's OK** ☐

_____ **1.** Verify drum brake problem concerns.

_____ Noise (describe) ______________________

_____ Poor stopping

_____ Pulling (toward which side?) ______________

_____ Grabbing (when?) ______________________

_____ Dragging

_____ Brake pedal pulsation

_____ **2.** Hoist the vehicle safely.

_____ **3.** Wet the brake drum or install a vacuum enclosure to provide protection against possible asbestos dust.

_____ **4.** Remove the brake drums.

_____ **5.** Describe the condition of the drum brake parts:

_____ Brake drum ______________________

_____ Lining ______________________

_____ Springs ______________________

_____ Self-adjuster ______________________

_____ Backing plate ______________________

_____ **6.** List the parts or service operation needed to restore the brakes to like-new condition.

____

____

Brake Drum Measurement

Meets NATEF Task: (A5-C-2) Inspect and Measure Brake Drums and Determine Necessary Action (P-1)

Name ________________________________ **Date** ________________________

Make/Model ___________________________ **Year** ________ **Instructor's OK** ☐

_____ **1.** Wet the brake drum or use an enclosure to help protect against asbestos exposure.

_____ **2.** Remove the brake drum from the vehicle and label the left and right to ensure that the drum is replaced in the original location.

_____ **2.** Thoroughly inspect the brake drum.

- Hot (hard) spots

  OK_____ **NOT OK**_____ (requires replacement)

- Tap with a hammer. The brake drum should ring like a bell if not cracked.

  OK_____ **NOT OK**_____ (requires replacement)

_____ **3.** Determine the maximum allowable inside diameter of the brake drum or the maximum "turn to" dimension.

Maximum allowable inside diameter = ___________ (allow 0.030" for wear)

Maximum "turn to" diameter = ___________

_____ **4.** Measure the drum using a drum micrometer.

Left = __________ Right = ___________

OK to machine ______ **NOT OK to machine** ______

Machining a Brake Drum

Meets NATEF Task: (A5-C-3) Refinish Brake Drum (P-1)

Name ________________________________ **Date** ______________________

Make/Model ________________________ **Year** ________ **Instructor's OK** ☐

_____ **1.** Measure the drum and double check that the brake drum can be safely machined.

- Maximum allowable inside diameter = ________
- Actual measurement of the drum = _____ left = _______ right = _______

OK to machine _______ **discard** ________

_____ **2.** Select the proper tapered centering cone and face supporting plate.

_____ **3.** Install a self-aligning spacer (SAS) and tighten the spindle nut.

_____ **4.** Perform a scratch cut.

_____ **5.** Stop the lathe, loosen the spindle nut, and rotate the brake drum 180° (one-half turn) and retighten the spindle nut.

_____ **6.** Perform a second scratch cut.

- If the second cut is in the same location, proceed with machining.
- If the second cut is on the opposite side of the drum, clean or repair the lathe before machining.

_____ **7.** Install a silencer band (vibration damper).

_____ **8.** Machine the drum.

_____ **9.** The measurement of the drum after machining = _________.

Does this allow 0.030" or more for wear?

Yes ____ (install on the vehicle) **No** ____ (replace the drum)

Drum Brake Inspection

Meets NATEF Task: (A5-C-4) Remove, Clean, Inspect Drum Brake Parts and Determine Necessary Action (P-1)

Name ________________________ **Date** ________________

Make/Model ____________________ **Year** ________ **Instructor's OK** [ ]

_____ **1.** Hoist the vehicle safely to a good working height (about chest high).

_____ **2.** Remove the rear wheels.

_____ **3.** Remove the brake drums (they should pull straight off - if you have problems, see the instructor).

_____ **4.** Check the thickness of the lining remaining. (The brake lining should show equal thickness on both shoes and have a minimum thickness equal to the thickness of a nickel.)

OK ____ **NOT OK** ____ **Describe any faults** ____________________

_____ **5.** Tap the brake drum with a steel hammer (it should ring like a bell)

OK ____ **NOT OK** ____ **(discard)**

_____ **6.** Measure the inside diameter of the drum and compare to the specifications.

Specifications = _______

Actual: left = _____ right = _____

OK ____ **NOT OK** ____

_____ **7.** Check for any brake fluid or rear axle fluid leakage.

OK ____ **NOT OK** ____

_____ **8.** Reinstall the drums.

_____ **9.** Install the wheels, torque the lug nuts, and lower the vehicle.

_____ **10.** Test drive the vehicle before returning it to the customer.

Drum Brake Overhaul

Meets NATEF Task: (A5-C-4) Remove, Clean, and Inspect Drum Brake Parts and Reassemble (P-1)

Name ________________________________ **Date** ________________________

Make/Model ____________________________ **Year** ________ **Instructor's OK** ☐

_____ **1.** Hoist the vehicle safely to a good working height (about chest high).

_____ **2.** Remove the rear wheels.

_____ **3.** Remove the brake drums.

_____ **4.** Carefully inspect the brake drum.

- Hot (hard) spots **OK**_____ **NOT OK**_____ (requires replacement)
- Tap with a hammer. The brake drum should ring like a bell if not cracked.

OK_____ **NOT OK**_____ (requires replacement)

_____ **5.** Measure the drum and replace or machine as necessary. replace ____ machine ____

_____ **6.** Remove the old brake lining and hardware.

_____ **7.** Clean, inspect, and lubricate the backing plate.

_____ **8.** Inspect and replace the wheel cylinder as necessary.

_____ **9.** Clean and lubricate the star-wheel adjuster.

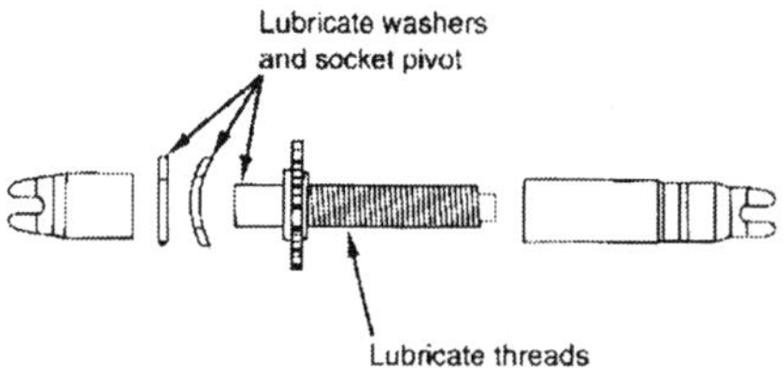

Lubricate washers and socket pivot

Lubricate threads

_____ **10.** Check or replace all hardware including the hold-down springs and return springs.

_____ **11.** Double check that the replacement brake shoes are the right size.

_____ **12.** Install the brake shoes, hardware, springs, and self adjuster.

_____ **13.** Adjust the brake shoes using a drum-shoe clearance gauge.

_____ **14.** Have the instructor check your work before installing the brake drum.

Instructor's OK ________________

_____ **15.** Install the brake drum, wheel, and torque the lug nuts.

_____ **16.** Repeat on the other side of the vehicle.

_____ **17.** Lower the vehicle and test drive the vehicle before returning it to the customer.

Dual Servo Drum Brake

Meets NATEF Task: (A5-C-4) Remove, Clean, and Inspect Drum Brake Parts and Reassemble (P-1)

Name ________________________________ **Date** ______________________

Make/Model ________________________ **Year** ________ **Instructor's OK** ☐

A dual servo (also called duo-servo) drum brake uses two brake shoes. The brake shoes attach to the wheel cylinder at the top and each other through an adjuster assembly at the bottom. The primary lining faces toward the front of the vehicle and use shorter linings than the rear (secondary) lining.

_____ **1.** Hoist the vehicle safely to a good working height (about chest high).

_____ **2.** Remove the rear wheels and brake drums.

_____ **3.** Machine or replace the brake drum as needed.

_____ **4.** Carefully clean the brake dust using an approved vacuum or liquid wash system.

_____ **5.** Remove the return springs, hold-down springs, self adjuster, and brakes shoes.

_____ **6.** Inspect the wheel cylinder and replace as necessary.

_____ **7.** Clean and lubricate the backing plate.

_____ **8.** Show the instructor the disassembled brake.

Instructor's OK _______

_____ **9.** Reassemble the brakes.

_____ **10.** Reinstall the brake drum and test the brakes for proper operation.

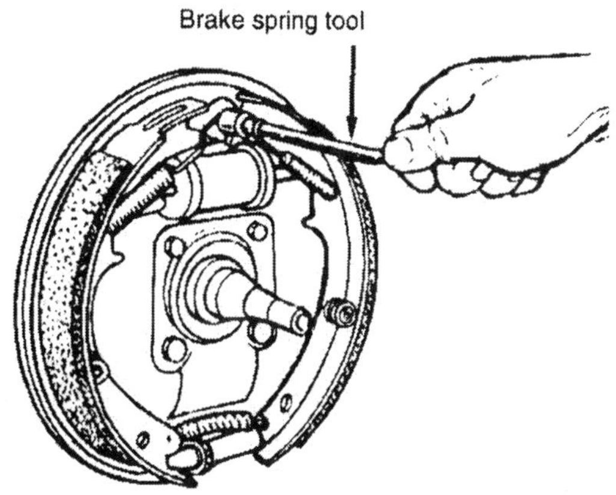

Leading/Trailing Drum Brake

Meets NATEF Task: (A5-C-4) Remove, Clean, and Inspect Drum Brake Parts and Reassemble (P-1)

Name ______________________________ **Date** ______________________

Make/Model __________________________ **Year** ________ **Instructor's OK** ☐

A leading/trailing drum brake uses two equal length brake shoes that are anchored at the bottom and attached to the wheel cylinder at the top.

_____ **1.** Hoist the vehicle safely to a good working height (about chest high).

_____ **2.** Remove the rear wheels and brake drums.

_____ **3.** Machine or replace the brake drum as needed.

_____ **4.** Carefully clean the brake dust using an approved vacuum or liquid wash system.

_____ **5.** Remove the return springs, hold-down springs, self adjuster, and brakes shoes.

_____ **6.** Inspect the wheel cylinder and replace as necessary.

_____ **7.** Clean and lubricate the backing plate.

_____ **8.** Show the instructor the disassembled brake.

Instructor's OK _______

_____ **9.** Reassemble the leading/ trailing brake.

_____ **10.** Reinstall the brake drum and test the brakes for proper operation.

Wheel Cylinder Inspection and Replacement

Meets NATEF Task: (A5-C-5) Remove, Inspect, and Install Wheel Cylinders (P-2)

Name ______________________________ **Date** ____________________

Make/Model ________________________ **Year** ________ **Instructor's OK** ☐

_____ **1.** Check the service information for the specified procedure for wheel cylinder replacement for the vehicle being serviced. ______________________________

_____ **2.** Hoist the vehicle safely to a good working height (about chest high).

_____ **3.** Remove the rear wheels and brake drums.

_____ **4.** Use a dull tool and lift the edge of the dust boots on the wheel cylinder.

_____ Brake fluid dripped out (requires overhaul or replacement)
_____ Dust boot is wet (normal, further inspection may be needed)
_____ Dust boot is dry (normal, further inspection may be needed)

_____ **5.** Remove the brake shoes to allow access to the wheel cylinders.

HINT: Some service technicians apply the parking brake to force the brake shoe away from the wheel cylinder providing the clearance necessary to remove or replace the wheel cylinder without having to remove the brake shoe.

_____ **6.** Remove the wheel cylinder from the backing plate and disassemble.

_____ **7.** Clean the wheel cylinder with denatured alcohol or brake cleaner.

_____ **8.** Clean and inspect the bore of the wheel cylinder.

_____ Slightly pitted (can usually be restored to useful service by using crocus cloth and brake fluid)

NOTE: Many vehicle manufacturers do not recommend using a cylinder hone because it would remove the special bearingized surface finish that is manufactured onto the inside surface of the wheel cylinder.

_____ Heavily pitted (most manufacturers recommend replacement only).

_____ **9.** After cleaning and inspection, do you overhaul or replace?

_____ Overhaul using new seals and boots

_____ Replacement with new wheel cylinders

_____ **10.** Reinstall the wheel cylinders, brake linings, drums, and bleed the system.

_____ **11.** Lower the vehicle and test drive before returning the vehicle to the customer.

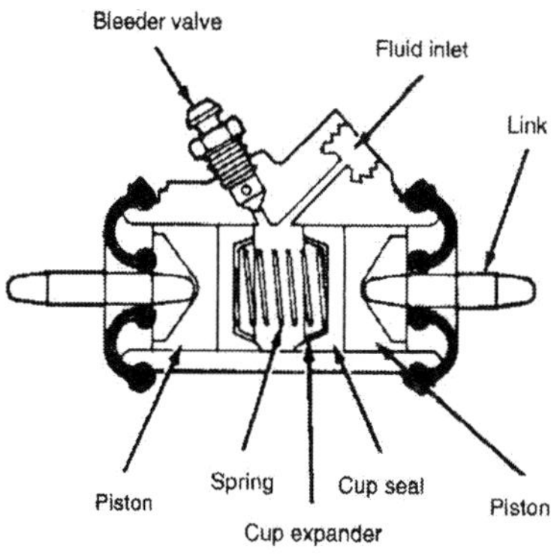

Pre-Adjustment of Brake Shoes

Meets NATEF Task: (A5-C-6) Pre-Adjust Brake Shoes (P-1)

Name ______________________ **Date** ______________________

Make/Model ______________________ **Year** ________ **Instructor's OK** ☐

Brake shoes should be pre-adjusted to close to the working clearance between the brake shoes and the brake drum before the brake drum is installed.

_____ **1.** Assemble the drum brake and verify that all parts are properly lubricated.

_____ **2.** Using a brake shoe clearance gauge, insert it into the drum and turn the lock knob to hold the setting.

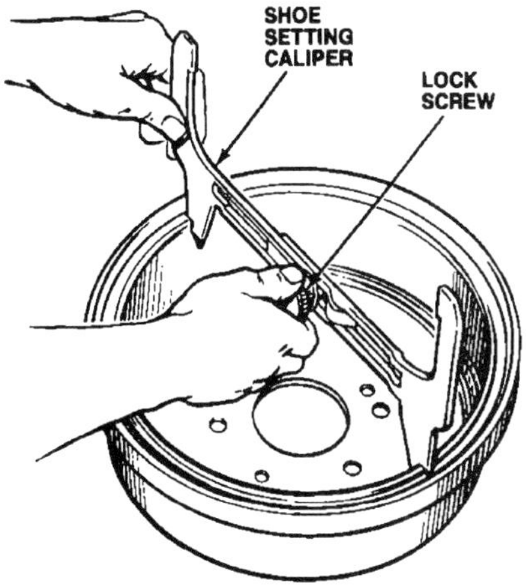

SHOE SETTING CALIPER

LOCK SCREW

_____ **3.** Install the brake shoe clearance gauge over the brake shoes and turn the adjuster until the lining contacts the gauge.

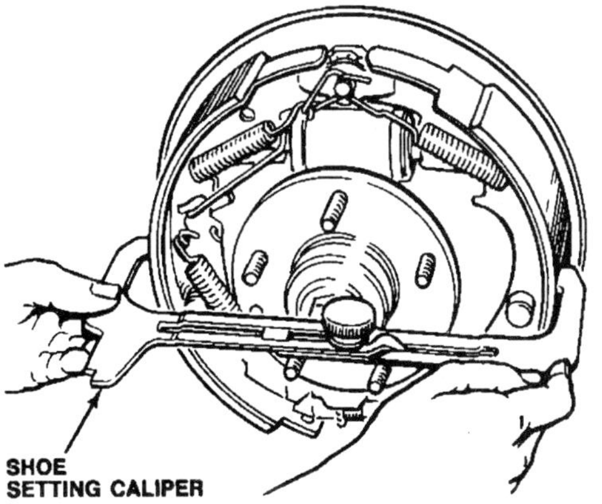

SHOE SETTING CALIPER

_____ **4.** Verify the pre-adjustment by installing the drum. It should slide over the brake shoes with little clearance.

OK ____ **NOT OK** ____

Torquing Wheel Lug Nuts

Meets NATEF Task: (A5-C-7) Install Wheel and Torque Lug Nuts (P-1)

Name ______________________________ **Date** ______________________

Make/Model ________________________ **Year** ________ **Instructor's OK** ☐

_____ **1.** Determine the vehicle manufacturer's specified lug nut torque specification.

__________ (usually between 80 and 100 lb-ft)

_____ **2.** Use a hand-operated wire brush on the wheel studs to ensure clean and dry threads and check for damage.

OK _____ **NOT OK** _____ Describe fault: ______________________

_____ **3.** Verify that the lug nuts are OK and free of defects.

_____ **4.** Install the wheel over the studs and start all lug nuts (or bolts) by hand.

_____ **5.** Tighten the lug nuts a little at a time in a star pattern using an air impact wrench equipped with the proper torque limiting adapter or a torque wrench.

_____ Used a torque wrench

_____ Used an air impact with a torque limiting adapter

_____ **6.** Tighten the lug nuts to final torque in a star pattern.

NOTE: "Tighten one, skip one, tighten one" is the usual method if four or five lug nuts are used.

Disc Brake Problem Diagnosis

Meets NATEF Task: (A5-D-1) Diagnosis and Inspection of Disc Brake Problems (P-1)

Name ______________________________ **Date** ______________________

Make/Model __________________________ **Year** ________ **Instructor's OK** [ ]

_____ **1.** Verify disc brake problem concerns.

_____ Noise (describe) ____________________________________

_____ Poor stopping

_____ Pulling (toward which side?) ___________________

_____ Grabbing (when?) ____________________________________

_____ Dragging

_____ Brake pedal pulsation

_____ **2.** Hoist the vehicle safely.

_____ **3.** Wet the brake caliper or install a vacuum enclosure to provide protection against possible asbestos dust.

_____ **4.** Remove the caliper from the mounting and carefully inspect for leaks of the caliper, pads, mounts, and hardware.

OK _____ **NOT OK** _____ Describe faults: ____________________

_____ **5.** Carefully inspect the caliper mounts for wear or damage. Lubricate as necessary.

_____ **6.** List the parts or service operation needed to restore the brakes to like-new condition.

____

____

Remove and Inspect Disc Brake Pads

Meets NATEF Task: (A5-D-4) Remove Clean, and Inspect Pads and Retaining Hardware; Determine Necessary Action (P-1)

Name ______________________________ **Date** ______________________

Make/Model ________________________ **Year** ________ **Instructor's OK** ☐

_____ **1.** Check the service information for the specified procedure for removing and reinstalling disc brake pads. ____

____

____

_____ **2.** The procedure usually includes the following steps.

A. Hoist the vehicle safely to a good working height.

B. Remove the wheels.

C. Remove the caliper retaining bolts and slide the caliper assembly off of the rotor.

NOTE: The caliper piston may need to be pushed into the caliper to provide the necessary clearance to remove the caliper from the rotor. Most vehicle manufacturers recommend that the bleeder valve be opened before the caliper piston is pushed inward to prevent brake fluid from being forced backward into the ABS hydraulic unit or master cylinder.

D. Remove the pads from the caliper and inspect them for wear, cracks, and chips. **OK** ____ **NOT OK** ____

_____ **3.** Based on the inspection, what is the necessary action?

____

____

____

____

Disc Brake Caliper Assembly

Meets NATEF Task: (A5-D-5) Reassemble, Lubricate and Reinstall the Calipers, Pads, and Related Hardware, Seat Pads, and Inspect for Leaks (P-1)

Name ______________________ **Date** ______________________

Make/Model ______________________ **Year** ________ **Instructor's OK** [ ]

_____ **1.** Check the service information for the specified procedure to follow for reassembly of the caliper assembly. ____

____

_____ **2.** The procedure usually includes the following steps.

A. Thoroughly clean the caliper using denatured alcohol.

B. Install new square-cut O-rings into the groove in the caliper bore and coat the bore and seal with clean brake fluid from a sealed container.

C. Lubricate the caliper piston with clean brake fluid and install the caliper piston dust boot on the piston and then install the piston into the bore.

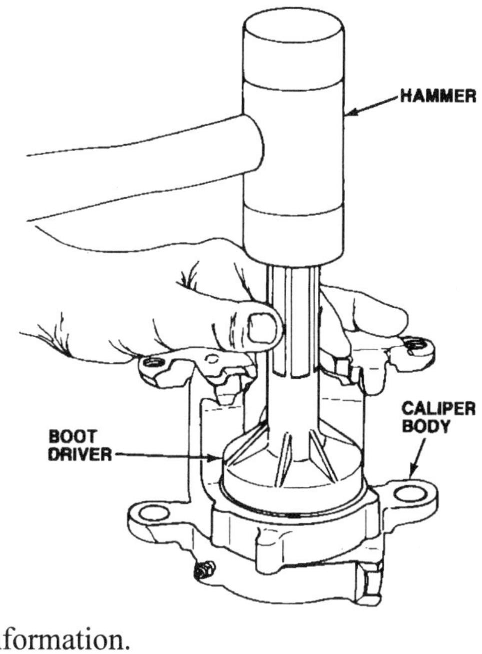

D. Seat the caliper piston dust seal.

E. Seat the pads as specified by the service information.

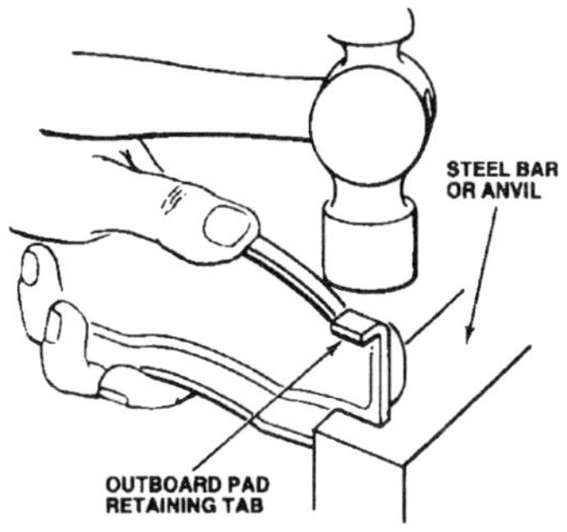

F. Install the caliper on the vehicle.

_____ **3.** After installation of the caliper and pads, bleed the system.

_____ **4.** Check for proper operation.

Front Disc Brake Inspection

Meets NATEF Task: (A5-D-2) Remove Caliper Assembly, Determine Necessary Action and Reassemble (P-1)

Name ______________________________ **Date** ______________________

Make/Model ___________________________ **Year** ________ **Instructor's OK** ☐

_____ **1.** Hoist the vehicle safely to a good working height (about chest high).

_____ **2.** Remove the front wheels.

_____ **3.** Loosen the bleeder valve and push the caliper piston into the caliper.

_____ **4.** Remove the caliper and pads.

_____ **5.** Check the front disc pad condition (the thickness of the friction material should be thicker than the metal part of the pads), and the thickness should be equal on both sides of the rotor.

OK ____ **NOT OK** ____ **Describe any faults** ____________________

_____ **6.** Check the rotors and measure the thickness and compare to the specifications.

Specifications = ________________

Actual: left = _______ right = _______

_____ 7. Check for brake fluid leaks and cracked flex hoses.

OK ____ **NOT OK** ____

_____ **8.** Reinstall the pads and caliper.

_____ **9.** Seat the pads.

_____ **10.** Lubricate the guide pins and rings.

_____ **11.** Tighten the bleeder valve.

_____ **12.** Depress the brake pedal several times to reset the pads.

_____ **13.** Install the wheels, torque the lug nuts, and lower the vehicle.

_____ **14.** Test drive the vehicle before returning it to the customer.

Disc Brake Caliper Overhaul

Meets NATEF Task: (A5-D-5) Disassemble and Clean Caliper Assembly, Replace Worn Parts (P-2)

Name ______________________________ **Date** ______________________

Make/Model ____________________________ **Year** ________ **Instructor's OK** [ ]

_____ **1.** Check the service information for the specified disc brake caliper overhaul procedure.

____

_____ **2.** Hoist the vehicle safely and remove the wheels.

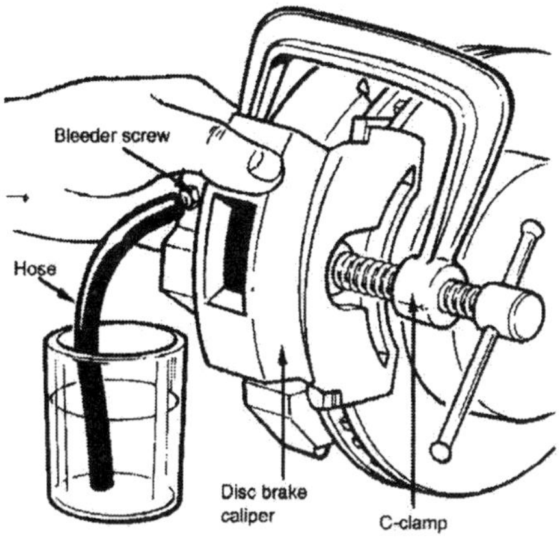

_____ **3.** Open the bleeder valve and compress the piston.

> **NOTE:** If the bleeder valve breaks or if the piston does not retract, consider replacing the caliper instead of overhauling it.

_____ **4.** Remove the brake line and the caliper assembly from the vehicle.

> **NOTE:** Remove one caliper at a time to avoid the possible problem of installing the caliper on the wrong side of the vehicle.

_____ **5.** Place a block of wood or a shop cloth beside the caliper piston and use compressed air to remove the piston, dust boot, and caliper O-ring.

_____ **6.** Clean the caliper assembly and piston.

_____**Piston OK** _____**Piston pitted**

_____ **7.** Thoroughly coat the new square-cut O-ring and install it in the groove in the caliper housing.

_____ **8.** Install the piston into the caliper.

_____ **9.** Install the caliper using new disc brake pads as necessary and new copper washers on both sides of the banjo bolt, if equipped.

_____ **10.** Bleed the caliper and repeat on the other side of the vehicle.

_____ **11.** Depress the brake pedal to ensure a firm brake pedal and test drive the vehicle before returning it to the customer.

Brake Rotor Measurement

Meets NATEF Task: (A5-D-7)Inspect and Measure Rotor with a Dial Indicator and Micrometer (P-1)

Name ______________________________ **Date** ____________________

Make/Model ____________________________ **Year** ________ **Instructor's OK** [ ]

_____ **1.** Visually inspect the brake rotor for:

- hard spots **OK** ___ **NOT OK** ___ (requires replacement)
- excessive rust **OK** ___ **NOT OK** ___
- deep grooves (over 0.060" deep) **OK** ___ **NOT OK** ___

_____ **2.** Check the service information and determine the specifications and measurements for thickness.

Minimum thickness = ________

Machine-to-thickness = ________

Actual thickness = _________ **OK** ___ **NOT OK** ___

_____ **3.** Determine the specifications for thickness variation (parallelism).

____

_____ **4.** Using a micrometer, measure the thickness at four or more locations around the rotor to determine the thickness variation (parallelism). (Usually 0.0005" or less difference in the readings.)

A. ________ C. ________ E. ________

B. ________ D. ________ F. ________

OK ___ **NOT OK** ___

_____ **5.** Use a dial indicator and measure the runout of the rotor.

Runout = ____________ (should be less than 0.005 in.)

OK ___ **NOT OK** ___

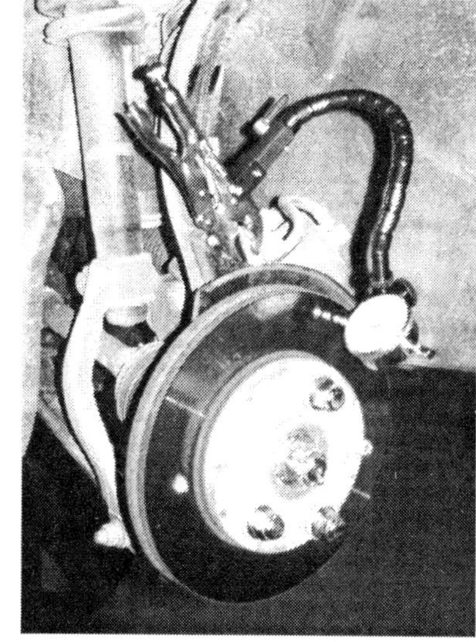

Remove and Replace a Disc Brake Rotor

Meets NATEF Task: (A5-D-8) Remove and Reinstall Rotor (P-1)

Name ________________________________ **Date** ______________________

Make/Model ___________________________ **Year** ________ **Instructor's OK** ☐

_____ **1.** Hoist the vehicle safely and remove the wheels.

_____ **2.** Wet the disc brake caliper and pads or install a vacuum enclosure to provide protection against possible asbestos dust.

_____ **3.** Remove the caliper retaining fasteners and remove the caliper assembly.

_____ **4.** Use a stiff wire and support the caliper.

CAUTION: Do not allow the caliper to hang by the flexible brake hose.

_____ **5.** Remove the disc brake rotor.

A. If a hub-type rotor, remove the dust cover, cotter pins, retaining nut, and remove the bearings and rotor from the spindle.
B. If a hubless rotor, remove the rotor from the hub.

_____ **6.** Clean the rotor contact surfaces.

_____ **7.** Reinstall the rotor. If a hub-type rotor, adjust the wheel bearing according to manufacturer's specifications.

_____ **8.** Reinstall the caliper assembly.

_____ **9.** Depress the brake pedal several times to restore proper braking action.

_____ **10.** Reinstall the wheels, torque the lug nuts to factory specifications, and lower the vehicle.

Machining a Brake Rotor

Meets NATEF Task: (A5-D-9) Refinish Rotor According to Manufacturer's Recommendations (P-1)

Name ______________________________ **Date** ____________________

Make/Model __________________________ **Year** ________ **Instructor's OK** ☐

_____ **1.** Carefully inspect the rotor for hot spots or damage.

OK _____ **NOT OK** _____ (requires replacement of the rotor)

_____ **2.** Determine minimum rotor thickness = ________ or machine to thickness = ________

_____ **3.** Measure the rotor thickness = _____. **OK to machine___ NOT OK to machine___**

_____ **4.** Clean the brake lathe spindle.

_____ **5.** Select the proper tapered cover and/or collets to properly secure the rotor to the lathe spindle.

_____ **6.** Install the self-aligning spacer (SAS) and tighten the spindle nut.

_____ **7.** Install the silencer band (noise damper).

_____ **8.** Perform a scratch test.

_____ **9.** Stop the lathe and loosen the spindle nut.

_____ **10.** Rotate the rotor 180° (one-half turn) and tighten the spindle nut.

_____ **11.** Perform another scratch cut. If the second scratch cut is in the same location as the first scratch cut or extends completely around the rotor, the machining of the rotor can continue. (If the second scratch cut is 180 from the first scratch cut, remove the rotor and clean the spindle and attaching hardware. Repeat the scratch test.)

_____ **12.** Machine the rotor removing as little material as possible.

_____ **13.** Measure the rotor with a micrometer to be sure rotor thickness is still within limits.

_____ **14.** Use 150 grit aluminum oxide sandpaper on a block of wood for 60 seconds on each side or a grinder to provide a smooth nondirectional finish.

_____ **15.** Thoroughly clean the rotor friction surface.

_____ **16.** Remove the rotor from the lathe.

On-the-Vehicle Lathe

Meets NATEF Task: (A5-D-9) Refinish Rotor According to Manufacturer's Recommendations (P-1)

Name ______________________________ **Date** ____________________

Make/Model __________________________ **Year** ________ **Instructor's OK** ☐

_____ **1.** Hoist the vehicle safely to the proper height according to the lathe manufacturer's instructions.

_____ **2.** Remove the front wheels.

_____ **3.** Mount the on-the-vehicle lathe according to the lathe manufacturer's instructions and calibrate the lathe as necessary.

> **NOTE:** On caliper mounted on-the-vehicle lathe, the disc brake caliper must be removed and supported with a wire to help prevent damage to the hydraulic flexible brake line.

_____ **4.** Machine the rotor following the lathe manufacturer's instructions.

_____ **5.** Use 150 grit aluminum oxide sandpaper on a block or a grinding disc to provide the required smooth non-directional finish.

_____ **6.** Disconnect and move the on-the-vehicle lathe to the other side of the vehicle and repeat steps 3 through 5 on the rotor on the other side of the vehicle.

_____ **7.** Thoroughly clean both disc brake rotors before installing the replacement disc brake pads and reinstalling the disc brake caliper.

> **NOTE:** Be sure to install all anti-noise shims and hardware.

_____ **8.** Bleed the brakes as necessary.

_____ **9.** Reinstall the front wheels and tighten the lug nuts in a star pattern (tighten one, skip one, etc.) using a torque wrench on a torque-limiting adjuster with an air impact wrench.

_____ **10.** Lower the vehicle and depress the brake pedal several times to achieve proper brake pedal height.

_____ **11.** Test drive the vehicle before returning the vehicle to the customer.

Rear Disc Parking Brake Adjustment

Meets NATEF Task: (A5-D-10) Adjust Calipers with Integrated Parking Brake (P-3)

Name ______________________________ **Date** ______________________

Make/Model ________________________ **Year** _______ **Instructor's OK** ☐

Many vehicles equipped with rear disc brakes use a mechanical activated parking brake that is integral with the caliper. Most are designed to be self-adjusting by adjusting when excessive brake pad to rotor clearance occurs.

_____ **1.** Check the service information for the specified rear disc brake parking brake adjustment procedure.

____

_____ **2.** Check the number of "clicks" of the parking brake.

_____ Number of clicks (should be between 3 and 10)

OK _____ **NOT OK** _____

If over 10 clicks is needed to set the parking brake, the rear disc brake caliper needs adjustment.

_____ **3.** Hoist the vehicle safely and remove both rear wheels.

_____ **4.** Carefully inspect the rear disc brakes for damage and measure the pads for excessive wear.

OK _____ **NOT OK** _____

Replace the pads if worn to the minimum allowable thickness.

_____ **5.** If the disc brake pads are serviceable, operate the parking brake lever using the appropriate size wrench on the actuating arm retaining bolt/nut while lightly tapping on the caliper using a dead blow plastic hammer. The adjusting mechanism should cause the piston to be repositioned with the correct pad to rotor clearance.

OK _____ **NOT OK** _____

If the proper clearance is not achieved, replacement of the calipers is required.

Vacuum Power Brake Booster Test

Meets NATEF Task: (A5-E-1 and 2) Test Vacuum Power Booster for Proper Operation and Vacuum (P-3)

Name ______________________________ **Date** ____________________

Make/Model __________________________ **Year** ________ **Instructor's OK** [ ]

_____ **1.** Check the service information for the specified procedure for testing a vacuum power brake booster for the vehicle being serviced.

____

_____ **2.** With the engine off, depress the brake pedal several times until the brake pedal feels hard (firm).

_____ **3.** The brake pedal should not fall to the floor of the vehicle.

OK _____ **NOT OK** _____

NOTE: If the brake pedal travels to the floor of the vehicle, carefully inspect the hydraulic brake system for a fault. Service or repair the hydraulic brake problem before continuing with this test.

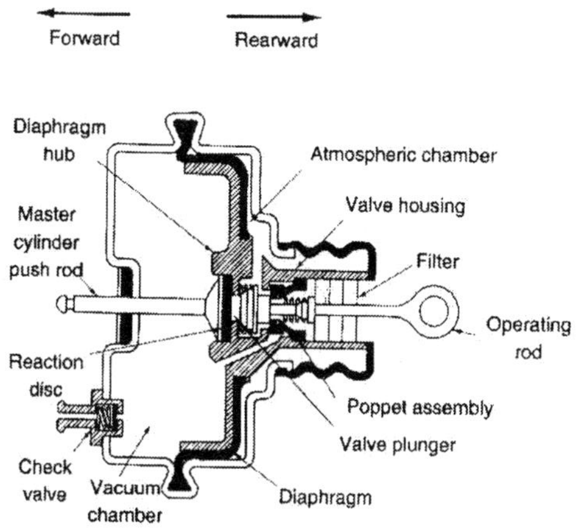

_____ **4.** With your foot still firmly depressing the brake pedal, start the engine. The brake pedal should go down.

OK _____ **NOT OK** _____

_____ **5.** If the brake pedal did not go down when the engine was started, visually check the following:

_____ Minimum of 15 in. Hg of vacuum to the vacuum booster from the engine manifold or auxiliary vacuum pump

_____ Proper operation of the one-way check valve

_____ Unrestricted charcoal filter between the booster and the intake manifold (if equipped)

_____ Inspect for vacuum leaks

OK _____ **NOT OK** _____

Hydro-Boost Test

Meets NATEF Task: (A5-E-4) Inspect and Test Hydro-Boost System for Leaks and Proper Operation (P-3)

Name ______________________________ **Date** ____________________

Make/Model ________________________ **Year** ________ **Instructor's OK** ☐

_____ **1.** Check the service information for the specified Hydro-Boost testing procedure for the vehicle being serviced.

____

_____ **2.** Start the testing of a Hydro-boost power brake assist system by carefully inspecting the following components:

Power steering fluid level	**OK** _____	**NOT OK** _____
Power steering pressure hoses for leaks	**OK** _____	**NOT OK** _____
Power steering pump drive belt	**OK** _____	**NOT OK** _____
Master cylinder brake fluid level	**OK** _____	**NOT OK** _____
Visually inspect the Hydro-boost assembly for evidence of power steering fluid leaks	**OK** _____	**NOT OK** _____

_____ **3.** Check the operation of the base hydraulic brakes by depressing the brake pedal several times with the engine "off" until the brake pedal feels firm. Continue to apply force to the brake pedal. The brake pedal should *not* drop.

OK _____ **NOT OK** _____(master cylinder or hydraulic system fault is indicated)

_____ **4.** With your foot still applying force to the brake pedal, start the engine. If the Hydro-boost system is functioning correctly, the brake pedal should drop.

OK _____ **NOT OK** _____

_____ **5.** To check the power steering pump for proper operation, connect a power steering pressure gauge or pressure and volume gauge between the pump and the Hydro-boost unit. Start the engine and observe the pressure and volume gauges.

Pressure at idle = _________
(should be less than 150 psi)
OK _____ **NOT OK** _____

Volume at idle = __________
(should be at least 2 gallons per minute)
OK _____ **NOT OK** _____

Wheel Bearing Diagnosis

Meets NATEF Task: (A5-F-1) Diagnose Wheel Bearing Noises, Wheel Shimmy, and Vibration Concerns (P-1)

Name ________________________________ **Date** ______________________

Make/Model ________________________ **Year** ________ **Instructor's OK** ☐

Worn or defective wheel bearings can cause a variety of concerns including:

Noise – usually a growl or rumble that changes tone with vehicle speed.

Wheel Shimmy – Can occur if the bearings are loose or excessively worn.

Vibration – Can occur if the bearings are loose or excessively worn.

_____ **1.** Drive the vehicle and check for abnormal noise that could be caused by a defective wheel bearing.

OK _____ **NOT OK** _____

HINT: A defective wheel bearing often sounds like a noisy winter tire but does not change tone when the vehicle is being driven over various road surfaces.

_____ **2.** Hoist the vehicle safely and check for excessive wheel bearing play and/or noise.

OK _____ **NOT OK** _____

Describe the faults and location: ______________________________

_____ **3.** Based on the diagnosis, what action is necessary? ______________________

____

____

Wheel Bearing Service

Meets NATEF Task: (A5-F-2) Remove, Clean, Inspect, Repack, and Install Wheel Bearings (P-1)

Name ______________________________ **Date** ____________________

Make/Model ________________________ **Year** ________ **Instructor's OK** ☐

_____ **1.** Remove the wheel cover and the hub dust cap (grease cap).

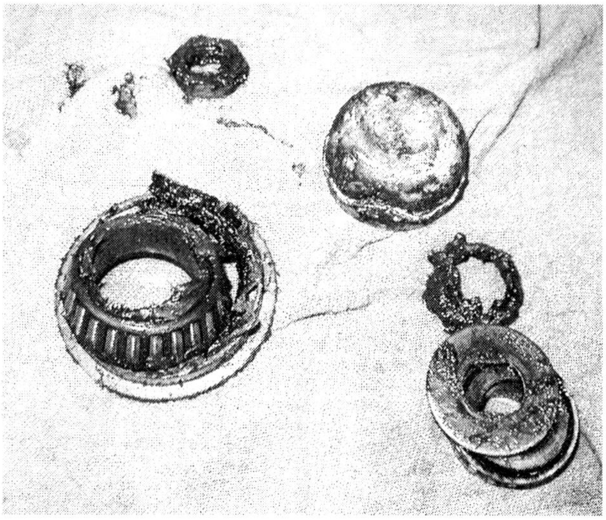

_____ **2.** Remove and discard the cotter key.

_____ **3.** Remove the spindle nut, washer and outer bearing.

_____ **4.** Remove inner and outer bearing and grease seal.

_____ **5.** Thoroughly clean the bearing in solvent and denatured alcohol or brake cleaner and blow it dry with compressed air.

_____ **6.** Closely inspect the bearing for wear or damage.

_____ **7.** Show the instructor the cleaned bearing. **Instructor's OK** ____________

_____ **8.** Repack the bearing with the correct type of wheel bearing grease.

_____ **9.** Install a new grease seal using a seal installing tool.

_____ **10.** Correctly adjust the bearing preload:

- ____ Install the spindle nut and while rotating the tire assembly, tighten (snug only, 12 to 30 lb.-ft.) with a wrench to "seat" the bearing correctly in the race.
- _____ While still rotating the tire assembly, loosen the nut approximately 1/2 turn and then *hand tighten only.*
- _____ Install a new cotter key (the common size is 1/8" diameter and 1.5 inches long).
- _____ Bend the ends of the cotter key up and around the nut to prevent interference with the dust cap.

_____ **11.** Install the hub dust cap (grease cap) and wheel cover.

Sealed Wheel Bearing Replacement

Meets NATEF Task: (A5-F-9) Remove and Install Sealed Wheel Bearing Assembly (P-2)

Name ______________________________ **Date** ____________________

Make/Model ________________________ **Year** ________ **Instructor's OK** [ ]

_____ **1.** Check service information for the specified replacement procedure for the vehicle being serviced. ____

_____ **2.** Remove the wheel cover.

_____ **3.** Loosen (do not remove) the drive axle shaft nut.

_____ **4.** Hoist the vehicle safely to a good working height (about chest high).

_____ **5.** Remove the front wheel.

_____ **6.** Use a steel drift between the caliper and the rotor cooling vent hole to hold the rotor from rotating.

_____ **7.** Remove the drive axle shaft hub nut.

_____ **8.** Remove the front disc brake caliper.

_____ **9.** Remove the rotor.

_____ **10.** Remove the hub and splash shield retaining bolts.

_____ **11.** Mark the location of the hub and make certain the hub is loose on the steering knuckle.

_____ **12.** Install the hub puller and remove the bearing and hub assembly.

_____ **13.** Clean and lubricate hub bearing surface.

_____ **14.** Reinstall the hub and bearing using the drive axle shaft nut. (Do not torque to the final setting, just until the hub is seated.)

_____ **15.** Reinstall the rotor, caliper, and wheel.

_____ **16.** Lower the vehicle and tighten the drive axle shaft nut to the final specification. Specification = ______________ (usually about 200 lb.-ft.)

Parking Brake Adjustment

Meets NATEF Task: (A5-F-3) Check Parking Brake Operation and Determine Necessary Action (P-1)

Name ______________________________ **Date** ______________________

Make/Model ________________________ **Year** ________ **Instructor's OK** [ ]

_____ **1.** Check the service information for the specified parking brake adjustment for the vehicle being serviced. ______________________________________

_____ **2.** Apply the parking brake and count the number of "clicks."

_____ less than 4 "clicks"
_____ 5 - 10 "clicks"
_____ over 10 "clicks"

NOTE: If there are less than 4 "clicks" or more than 10 "clicks", adjustment of the parking brake may be necessary.

_____ **3.** Place the gear selector in neutral and release the parking brake.

_____ **4.** Hoist the vehicle safely.

_____ **5.** Try rotating the rear wheels (front wheels on some Subaru vehicles).

_____ rotates freely

_____ does not rotate

NOTE: If the rear wheels do not rotate, try loosening the parking brake cable.

_____ **6.** If the rear wheels rotate freely and the parking brake requires more than 10 "clicks," remove the rear brakes for inspection.

NOTE: The parking brake should only be adjusted after checking and adjusting the rear brakes.

_____ **7.** Clean and adjust the rear brakes.

_____ **8.** Reassemble the rear brakes and apply the parking brake 3 - 4 "clicks."

_____ **9.** If the rear wheels can be rotated, adjust the parking brake adjuster until the rear wheel brakes are just touching the brake drums.

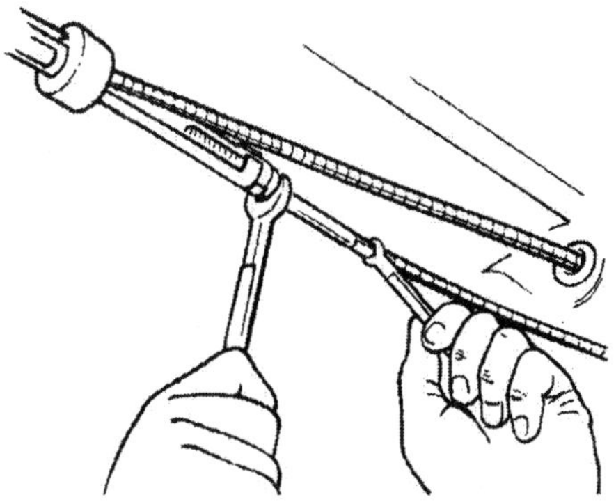

_____ **10.** Apply the parking brake and again count the "clicks." Most vehicle manufacturers recommend that the parking brake should hold with 6 to 18 "clicks." Readjust the parking brake as necessary.

Brake Stop Light Switch

Meets NATEF Task: (A5-F-6) Check Operation of Brake Stop Light System and Determine Necessary Action (P-1)

Name ______________________________ **Date** ______________________

Make/Model ________________________ **Year** ________ **Instructor's OK** ☐

_____ **1.** Check the service information for the specified testing procedures to determine the proper operation and adjustment of the brake stop light switch. _______________

____

____

_____ **2.** Check for the proper operation of the brake (stop) lights including the center high-mounted stop light (CHMSL).

OK ____ **NOT OK** ____

If not OK, determine the necessary action needed to restore proper operation.

____

____

_____ **3.** Describe the location of the brake switch ______________________________

_____ **4.** Describe how to adjust the brake switch (if adjustable) ____________________

____

_____ **5.** List the trade number of the brake light bulbs, including the center high-mounted stop light.

Rear brake light trade number = _______________

Center high-mounted stop light trade number = _______________

Wheel Bearing and Race Replacement

Meets NATEF Task: (A5-F-7) Replace Wheel Bearing and Race (P-1)

Name ______________________________ **Date** ______________________

Make/Model __________________________ **Year** ________ **Instructor's OK** ☐

_____ **1.** Remove the wheel cover and the hub dust cap (grease cap).

_____ **2.** Remove and discard the cotter key.

_____ **3.** Remove the spindle nut, washer and outer bearing.

_____ **4.** Remove inner and outer bearing and grease seal.

_____ **5.** Remove the bearing race using the specified tool.

_____ **6.** Show the instructor the removed race. **Instructor's OK** ______________

_____ **7.** Install new race using the correct bearing race installation tool.

_____ **8.** Show the instructor the new race. **Instructor's OK** ______________

_____ **9.** Install a new grease seal using a seal installing tool.

_____ **10.** Pack the new bearing with the correct type of wheel bearing grease.

_____ **11.** Correctly adjust the bearing preload:

____ Install the spindle nut and while rotating the tire assembly, tighten (snug only, 12 to 30 lb.-ft.) with a wrench to "seat" the bearing correctly in the race.

_____ While still rotating the tire assembly, loosen the nut approximately 1/2 turn and then *hand tighten only*.

_____ Install a new cotter key (the common size is 1/8" diameter and 1.5 inches long).

_____ Bend the ends of the cotter key up and around the nut to prevent interference with the dust cap.

_____ **12.** Install the hub dust cap (grease cap) and wheel cover.

Inspect and Replace Wheel Studs

Meets NATEF Task: (A5-F-8) Inspect and Replace Wheel Studs (P-1)

Name ______________________________ **Date** ______________________

Make/Model __________________________ **Year** ________ **Instructor's OK** ☐

_____ **1.** Hoist the vehicle safely.

_____ **2.** Remove all four wheels.

_____ **3.** Carefully inspect the wheel studs for excessive rust or damage.

LF = OK _____ **NOT OK** _____ Describe fault ____________________

RF = OK _____ **NOT OK** _____ Describe fault ____________________

LR = OK _____ **NOT OK** _____ Describe fault ____________________

RR = OK _____ **NOT OK** _____ Describe fault ____________________

_____ **4.** Clean the threads using a stiff wire brush.

CAUTION: Many vehicle manufacturers specify that grease or oil should *not* be used on the threads of wheel studs. If a lubricant is used on the threads, the lug nuts could loosen during vehicle operation, which could cause a wheel to fall off resulting in a collision and possible personal injury.

_____ **5.** Worn or damaged studs should be replaced. Check the service information for the specified procedure for replacing wheel studs on the vehicle being serviced.

____

_____ **6.** Which stud(s) were replaced? ________________________________

ABS and Traction Control Identification

Meets NATEF Task: (A5-G-1) Identify Antilock System Components (P-1)

Name ______________________________ **Date** ______________________

Make/Model ______________________ **Year** ________ **Instructor's OK** ☐

_____ **1.** Integral? ______ Nonintegral? _______

_____ **2.** List the number and locations of the wheel speed sensors.

Number = _________

Locations (describe) ______________________________________

_____ **3.** Check the number of channels:

One (rear-wheel only) _____

Three channels _____

Four channels _____

Unknown _____

_____ **4.** How many accumulators?

____ zero ____ one ____ two

____ other (describe) ______________________________________

_____ **5.** Describe the bleeding procedure (see service information): ____________

____

____

_____ **6.** Describe the diagnostic trouble code retrieval method: ______________

____

____

_____ **7.** What are the wheel speed sensor specifications? (See service information.)

Front = ________________ Adjustable? _____ Specs. __________

Rear = ________________ Adjustable? _____ Specs. __________

_____ **8.** Equipped with traction control? **Yes** _____ **No** _____

Diagnose ABS System Concerns

Meets NATEF Task: (A5-G-2) Diagnose ABS Operational Concerns and Determine Necessary Action (P-2)

Name ______________________________ **Date** ______________________

Make/Model ____________________________ **Year** ________ **Instructor's OK** [ ]

_____ 1. **Poor stopping** – Check the following system or components.

A. Tires – condition and sizes **OK** _____ **NOT OK** _____

B. Base brake components such as calipers, pads, and drive brake components

OK _____ **NOT OK** _____

_____ 2. **Abnormal pedal feel or pulsation** – Check the following components.

A. Wheel speed sensor tone ring or wiring for damage.

OK _____ **NOT OK** _____

B. Brake rotors and drum for out-of-round or other faults

OK _____ **NOT OK** _____

C. Master cylinder and brake fluid for level or contaminants

OK _____ **NOT OK** _____

_____ 3. **Wheel lockup** – Check the following components.

A. Base brake friction material (pads and linings) for grease, excessive wear or contamination.

OK _____ **NOT OK** _____

B. Wheel speed sensor tone ring for damage

OK _____ **NOT OK** _____

C. Excessively worn or mismatched tires

OK _____ **NOT OK** _____

_____ 4. **Abnormal noise** – Check the following components.

A. Accumulator leakage creating the need for extended pump operation

OK _____ **NOT OK** _____

B. Base brakes for excessive wear or defective friction components

OK _____ **NOT OK** _____

ABS Component Inspection

Meets NATEF Task: (A5-G-1) Inspect ABS Component and Determine Needed Action (P-1)

Name ______________________________ **Date** ____________________

Make/Model ____________________________ **Year** _________ **Instructor's OK** ☐

_____ **1.** Check the brake fluid level and condition in the master cylinder.

OK _____ **NOT OK** _____ **Describe** ______________________________

_____ **2.** Check the brake fluid level and condition in the ABS reservoir if equipped.

_____ Not equipped with an ABS brake fluid reservoir

OK _____ **NOT OK** _____ **Describe** ______________________________

_____ **3.** Visually check the hydraulic control unit and accumulator for leakage or physical damage.

OK _____ **NOT OK** _____ **Describe** ______________________________

_____ **4.** Visually check all wheel speed sensors and tone wheel for damage or debris.

OK _____ **NOT OK** _____ **Describe** ______________________________

_____ **5.** Visually inspect the wheel speed sensor wiring harness for damage.

OK _____ **NOT OK** _____ **Describe** ______________________________

_____ **6.** Visually inspect the ABS controller for damage or corroded connection(s).

OK _____ **NOT OK** _____ **Describe** ______________________________

ABS Code Retrieval and Erase

Meets NATEF Task: (A5-G-3) Diagnose ABS Electronic Control and Component Using Self Diagnosis (P-1)

Name ______________________________ **Date** ______________________

Make/Model ______________________ **Year** _______ **Instructor's OK** ☐

The purpose of this worksheet is to become familiar with how to retrieve diagnostic trouble codes (DTCs) and how to correctly erase stored DTCs.

_____ **1.** Identify the brand of ABS system by using the service information.

ABS (brand) = ____________________

_____ **2.** Describe the specified method to retrieve an ABS diagnostic trouble code (DTC):

____

____

_____ **3.** Set a code by disconnecting a relay or other easily reached component.

Component unplugged is ________________________

_____ **4.** Did a diagnostic trouble code set? **Yes** ____ **No** ____

_____ **5.** Retrieve the code. What code set? ______________________

_____ **6.** Did more than one code set? **Yes** ____ **No** ____

_____ **7.** Reconnect the relay or component.

_____ **8.** Describe the specified method to use to clear a stored diagnostic trouble code:

____

____

ABS Set a Code/Retrieve a Code

Meets NATEF Task: (A5-G-3) Diagnose ABS Electronic Control and Components Using Recommended Test Equipment (P-1)

Name ______________________________ **Date** ______________________

Make/Model ________________________ **Year** ________ **Instructor's OK** ☐

The purpose of this worksheet is to become familiar with how an ABS diagnostic trouble code (DTC) is set and how to retrieve the code.

_____ **1.** Disconnect a wheel speed sensor at the connector or electro-hydraulic unit.

_____ **2.** Start the engine (or drive the vehicle) until the amber ABS malfunction indicator lamp on the dash comes on.

_____ **3.** What method was used to retrieve the DTC?

____ scan tool

____ flash code ("key" or jumper wire)

____ other (describe) ______________________________

_____ **4.** What DTCs were set?

DTC # __________ What is the meaning of this code? ____________________

DTC # __________ What is the meaning of this code? ____________________

_____ **5.** Reconnect the wheel speed sensor or electro-mechanical electrical connector.

_____ **6.** What method is recommended to clear the DTCs? ______________________

____

_____ **7.** Retest the vehicle checking for proper brake and ABS operation.

ABS Wheel Speed Sensor Testing

Meets NATEF Task: (A5-G-7) Test, Diagnose, and Service ABS Wheel Speed Sensors (P-1)

Name ______________________________ **Date** ______________________

Make/Model ________________________ **Year** ________ **Instructor's OK** ☐

A magnetic wheel speed sensor can fail in a variety of ways including: electrically shorted, open, or grounded.

_____ **1.** Locate and disconnect the wheel speed sensor connector. Hoist the vehicle if necessary.

_____ **2.** Disconnect the wheel speed sensor (WSS) connector and connect a digital meter set to read ohms.

_____ **3.** Measure the resistance at the sensor terminals.

WSS resistance = ________

Compare the resistance to the factory specifications = __________ (usually about 1000 ohms).

OK _____ **NOT OK** _____

_____ **4.** With the meter still set to read ohms, connect one meter lead to a good clean chassis ground and the other lead to one terminal of the WSS connector. This test determines that the WSS is shorted to ground unless the meter indicates infinity (OL).

Meter reading = _____ should be infinity (OL). **OK** _____ **NOT OK** _____

_____ **5.** Set the digital meter to read AC volts.

_____ **6.** Connect the leads of the meter to the terminals of the wheel speed sensor.

_____ **7.** Have an assistant spin the wheel and observe the AC voltage on the meter display.

Reading = ________ AC volts (should be over 0.1 V (100 mV)

OK _____ **NOT OK** _____

_____ **8.** Observe the wheel speed sensor using a graphing multimeter (GMM) or a digital storage oscilloscope (DSO). Draw the waveform displayed while an assistant spins the wheel.

Depressurization of High-Pressure ABS

Meets NATEF Task: (A5-G-4) Depressurize High-Pressure ABS Components (P-3)

Name ______________________________ **Date** ______________________

Make/Model __________________________ **Year** ________ **Instructor's OK** [ ]

Integral ABS systems combine the function of the master cylinder, power-assist booster, and antilock brake functions in one assembly. These assemblies operate at high pressure and must be depressurized before performing service work on the brake system to avoid possible personal injury.

_____ **1.** Check the service information for the specified depressurization procedure for the vehicle being serviced.

____

_____ **2.** Visually check the brake fluid reservoir.

Proper level? **OK** _____ **NOT OK** _____

Brake fluid condition? Describe: ______________________________

_____ **3.** Inspect the ABS hydraulic control unit for signs of damage or leakage.

OK _____ **NOT OK** _____

_____ **4.** With the ignition key off, depress the brake pedal forty (40) times. The brake pedal should be hard when depressed after the first few brake applications

OK _____ **NOT OK** _____

If the brake pedal is not hard and a power-assisted brake application is still possible, find and correct the ignition feed circuit to the hydraulic control unit before proceeding to brake system service.

Bleed ABS Hydraulic Circuits

Meets NATEF Task: (A5-G-5) Bleed ABS Hydraulic Circuits (P-2)

Name ______________________________ **Date** ______________________

Make/Model ________________________ **Year** ________ **Instructor's OK** ☐

ABS hydraulic front and rear hydraulic circuits must be bled using the exact procedure specified by the vehicle manufacturer.

_____ **1.** Type of ABS system? _____ Integral or _____ non-integral

_____ **2.** Check the service information and state the vehicle manufacturer's specified bleeding procedure and sequence.

____

____

____

____

_____ **4.** Type of brake fluid specified for use during the bleeding procedure?

____

_____ **5.** Was a scan tool required? ____ **Yes** ____ **No** If yes, describe the procedure:

____

_____ **6.** Was a special tool or tools required? ____ **Yes** ____ No If yes, describe the procedure:

____

Remove and Install ABS Components

Meets NATEF Task: (A5-G-6) Remove and Install ABS Components (P-3)

Name ________________________________ **Date** ________________________

Make/Model ____________________________ **Year** ________ **Instructor's OK** [ ]

_____ **1.** Describe an ABS fault that requires the replacement of the ABS component if applicable.

____

____

____

_____ **2.** What unit/component is to be removed and installed?

____

_____ **3.** State the vehicle manufacturer's specified removal and reinstallation procedure.

____

____

____

_____ **4.** List the cautions and warnings that were included in the service procedure.

____

____

_____ **5.** Time needed to perform this operation? ____________________________

_____ **6.** Describe any problems encountered during this procedure.

____

____

____

Modified Vehicle ABS Problem Diagnosis

Meets NATEF Task: (A5-G-8) Diagnose ABS Concerns Due to Vehicle Modifications (P-3)

Name ______________________________ **Date** ______________________

Make/Model ________________________ **Year** ________ **Instructor's OK** [ ]

_____ **1.** Carefully inspect the vehicle for modifications such as changes made to wheels/tires, axle ratio, and curb height.

Tire size: **OK** _____ **NOT OK** _____ (describe) ____________________

Curb (ride) height: ___ stock ___ higher ___ lower (describe) ____________

Axle ratio: ___ stock ___ unknown (describe) ______________________

_____ **2.** Be sure that all four tires are the same size and brand.

LF tire size = __________ Brand = ________________________

RF tire size = __________ Brand = ________________________

RR tire size = __________ Brand = ________________________

LR tire size = __________ Brand = ________________________

_____ **3.** Did any of the modifications affect the braking?

___ **Yes**

___ **No** (describe) ____

_____ **4.** Did the modifications set an ABS diagnostic trouble code (DTC)?

___ **Yes** (describe) ____

___ **No**

_____ **5.** Check the service information and record the specified procedure to follow when servicing an antilock brake system on a vehicle that has been modified.

____

____

Suspension Problem Diagnosis

Meets NATEF Task: (A4-A-1) Identify and Interpret Suspension Concerns; Determine Necessary Action (P-1)

Name ______________________________ **Date** ______________________

Make/Model ________________________ **Year** ________ **Instructor's OK** ☐

_____ **1.** What is the stated customer concern? ______________________________

_____ **2.** Test drive the vehicle under the same conditions and road surface types as stated by the customer when the problem occurs and check the following.

Tire-type noise?	**OK** ____	**NOT OK** ____
Clunks?	**OK** ____	**NOT OK** ____
Creaks?	**OK** ____	**NOT OK** ____
Tracks straight?	**OK** ____	**NOT OK** ____
Pull during braking only?	**OK** ____	**NOT OK** ____
Wandering (unstable)?	**OK** ____	**NOT OK** ____

Other concern (describe) ______________________________

_____ **3.** When does the fault or concern occur?

- ___ During turns or cornering to the right
- ___ During turns or cornering to the left
- ___ During turns or cornering both to the right or the left
- ___ While driving straight ahead
- ___ Only when driving on a rough road
- ___ Only when turning into or out of a driveway
- ___ Other (describe) ______________________________

_____ **4.** Based on the test drive, what components or systems could be the cause of the suspension problem or concern?

____

____

_____ **5.** What action will be needed to correct these concerns? ____________________

____

____

Steering Problem Diagnosis

Meets NATEF Task: (A4-A-1) Identify and Interpret Steering Concerns; Determine Necessary Action (P-1)

Name ________________________________ **Date** ______________________

Make/Model ____________________________ **Year** ________ **Instructor's OK** [ ]

_____ **1.** What is the stated customer concern? ________________________________

_____ **2.** Test drive the vehicle under the same condition and road surface types as stated by the customer when the problem occurs and check the following.

Steers straight?	**OK** ____	**NOT OK** ____
Wanders?	**OK** ____	**NOT OK** ____
Noise during turns or corners?	**OK** ____	**NOT OK** ____
Hard steering when cold only?	**OK** ____	**NOT OK** ____
Hard steering when raining?	**OK** ____	**NOT OK** ____
Noise when steering?	**OK** ____	**NOT OK** ____
Looseness in steering wheel?	**OK** ____	**NOT OK** ____
Lack of steering control?	**OK** ____	**NOT OK** ____

Other concerns (describe) ________________________________

____

_____ **3.** When does the fault or concern occur?

___ During turns or cornering to the right
___ During turns or cornering to the left
___ During turns or cornering both to the right or the left
___ While driving straight ahead
___ Only when driving on a rough road
___ Only when turning into or out of a driveway
___ Other (describe) ________________________________

_____ **4.** Based on the test drive, what components or systems could be the cause of the suspension problem or concern?

____

____

_____ **5.** What action will be needed to correct these concerns? ____________________

____

____

Suspension and Steering System Information

Meets NATEF Task: (A4-A-2) Research Vehicle Information (P-1)

Name ______________________ **Date** ______________________

Make/Model ______________________ **Year** ________ **Instructor's OK** ☐

Consult the service information and determine the following.

_____ **1.** List suspension-related technician service bulletins (TSBs).

A. Topic ______________________ Bulletin Number ______________

Fault/Concern ____

Corrective Action ____

B. Topic ______________________ Bulletin Number ______________

Fault/Concern ____

Corrective Action ____

_____ **2.** List all published service precautions from the service information.

____

____

_____ **3.** Research the vehicle's service history and record all suspension or steering service or repairs.

____

____

_____ **4.** Record all suspension and steering specifications.

____

____

Disable/Enable Airbag Systems

Meets NATEF Task: (A4-B-1) Disable and Enable Supplemental Restraint System (P-1)

Name ______________________________ **Date** ______________________

Make/Model ________________________ **Year** ________ **Instructor's OK** [ ]

_____ **1.** Check the vehicle information for the specified steps and procedures that should be followed to disable and enable the supplemental restraint (airbag) system on the vehicle being serviced.

____

____

____

_____ **2.** Check all of the steps that are recommended.

___ Disconnect the battery negative cable
___ Remove the airbag circuit fuse
___ Disconnect the connector at the base of the steering column
___ Disconnect the connector for the passenger side airbag
___ Install the airbag inflator module load tool
___ Other (describe) ______________________________

_____ **3.** List the precautions stated in the service information when performing service work to the steering or suspension system around the components of the supplemental restraint system.

____

____

____

Airbag System Coil (Clock Spring)

Meets NATEF Task: (A4-B-2) Steering Wheel Removal and Centering of SRS Coil (Clock Spring (P-1)

Name ______________________ **Date** ______________________

Make/Model ______________________ **Year** ________ **Instructor's OK** ☐

_____ **1.** Consult the service information and determine the specified procedures needed to remove and replace the steering wheel and to center/time the supplemental restraint system (SRS) coil (clock spring).

____

____

____

____

____

_____ **2.** List the tools or equipment needed.

A. ____

B. ____

C. ____

D. ____

_____ **3.** List the safety precautions that are listed in the service information regarding these procedures.

A. ____

B. ____

C. ____

D. ____

Steering Column Problem Diagnosis

Meets NATEF Task: (A4-B-3) Diagnose Steering Column Noises, Looseness, and Binding Concerns and Determine Necessary Action (P-2)

Name ______________________________ **Date** ______________________

Make/Model ________________________ **Year** ________ **Instructor's OK** [ ]

_____ **1.** With the ignition key in the ignition (key on, engine off) and the steering column unlocked, rotate the steering wheel.

Steering wheel turns without noise	**OK** ____	**NOT OK** ____
Steering wheel does not turn – still locked	**OK** ____	**NOT OK** ____

_____ **2.** Check the service information and determine what service work is needed to correct?

____

____

_____ **3.** If equipped, check for proper operation of the tilt and telescopic functions of the steering column.

Works without excessive effort or looseness	**OK** ____	**NOT OK** ____
Does not work	**OK** ____	**NOT OK** ____
Works but is difficult to move or makes noise	**OK** ____	**NOT OK** ____
Works but has looseness in the column	**OK** ____	**NOT OK** ____

_____ **4.** Test drive the vehicle and determine if the steering column is loose or makes noise during normal driving.

OK ____ **NOT OK** ____

_____ **5.** After the analysis, what service procedures should be performed to restore the proper operation of the steering column?

____

____

Diagnose Power Steering Gear Problems

Meets NATEF Task: (A4-B-4) Diagnose Power Steering Gear Problems and Determine Necessary Action (P-3)

Name ________________________________ **Date** ______________________

Make/Model ___________________________ **Year** ________ **Instructor's OK** ☐

_____ **1.** Start the engine and turn the steering wheel full left and full right. Check the following items that apply.

OK ____ **NOT OK** ____ Steering feels and operates as normal without any abnormal noise, looseness, or binding.

OK ____ **NOT OK** ____ Steering wheel is difficult to turn.

OK ____ **NOT OK** ____ Steering feels loose or binds.

_____ **2.** Perform a visual inspection of the power steering pump and steering gear and check all that apply.

OK ____ **NOT OK** ____ No leaks and drive belt appears to be serviceable.

OK ____ **NOT OK** ____ Leak(s) detected. Describe the location _______
____

OK ____ **NOT OK** ____ Drive belt loose, defective, or worn. Describe the fault ________________________________

_____ **3.** Test drive the vehicle and describe the operation of the power steering. _________

____

____

_____ **4.** What actions are needed to correct the concern? ____________________________

____

____

Power Steering System Test

Meets NATEF Task: (A4-B-4) Diagnose Power Steering and Determine Necessary Action (P-3)

Name ______________________________ **Date** ______________________

Make/Model __________________________ **Year** _______ **Instructor's OK** ☐

(Using a Power Steering Pressure Tester)

Check the service information and/or pressure tester instructions for the exact test procedure.

A typical procedure includes:

_____ **1.** Start the engine. Allow the power steering system to reach operating temperatures.

_____ **2.** The pressure gauge should register 80 - 125 psi. If the pressure is greater than 150 psi, check for restrictions in the system including the operation of the poppet valve located in the inlet of the steering gear.

_____ **3.** Fully close the valve 3 times. All three readings should be within 50 psi of each other and the peak pressure higher than 1,000 psi.

NOTE: Do not leave the valve closed for more than 5 seconds!

_____ **4.** If the pressure readings are high enough *and* within 50 psi of each other, the pump is okay.

_____ **5.** If the pressure readings are high enough, yet not within 50 psi of each other, the flow control valve is sticking.

_____ **6.** If the pressure readings are less than 1,000 psi, replace the flow control valve and recheck. If the pressures are still low, replace the rotor and vanes in the power steering pump.

_____ **7.** If the pump is okay, turn the steering wheel to both stops. If the pressure at both stops is not the same as the maximum pressure, the steering gear (or rack and pinion) is leaking internally. **OK** ____ **NOT OK** ____

_____ **8.** If not OK, what action is needed to restore proper operation?

____

Diagnose Power Rack and Pinion Steering

Meets NATEF Task: (A4-B-5) Diagnose Power Rack and Pinion Steering Gear Problems and Determine Necessary Action (P-3)

Name ______________________________ **Date** ____________________

Make/Model ________________________ **Year** ________ **Instructor's OK** [ ]

_____ **1.** Start the engine and turn the steering wheel full left and full right. Check the following items that apply.

OK ____ **NOT OK** ____ Steering feels and operates as normal without any abnormal noise, looseness, or binding.

OK ____ **NOT OK** ____ Steering wheel is difficult to turn.

OK ____ **NOT OK** ____ Steering feels loose or binds.

_____ **2.** Perform a visual inspection of the power steering pump and steering gear and check all that apply.

OK ____ **NOT OK** ____ No leaks and drive belt appears to be serviceable.

OK ____ **NOT OK** ____ Leak(s) detected. Describe the location _______

____

OK ____ **NOT OK** ____ Drive belt loose, defective, or worn. Describe the fault ______________________________

_____ **3.** Test drive the vehicle and describe the operation of the power steering. _________

____

____

_____ **4.** What actions are needed to correct the concern? ___________________________

____

____

Steering Column Related Inspection

Meets NATEF Task: (A4-B-6) Inspect Steering U-Joints, Flexible Coupling(s) and Lock Cylinder Mechanism, and Steering Wheel; Perform Necessary Action (P-2)

Name ______________________________ **Date** ______________________

Make/Model ________________________ **Year** ________ **Instructor's OK** ☐

_____ **1.** Start the engine and turn the steering wheel full left and full right. Check the following items that apply.

OK ____ **NOT OK** ____ Steering wheel is difficult to turn.
OK ____ **NOT OK** ____ Steering feels loose or binds.
OK ____ **NOT OK** ____ Steering feels and operates as normal without any abnormal noise, looseness, or binding.

_____ **2.** Perform a visual inspection and check the flexible coupling and intermediate shaft for excessive wear or damage.

OK ____ **NOT OK** ____ Describe fault ______________________________

_____ **3.** Check the operation of the lock cylinder.

____ Works smoothly
____ Key is difficult to remove/or install
____ Other concern (describe) ______________________________

_____ **4.** Check the service information and determine needed action. ____________________

____

____

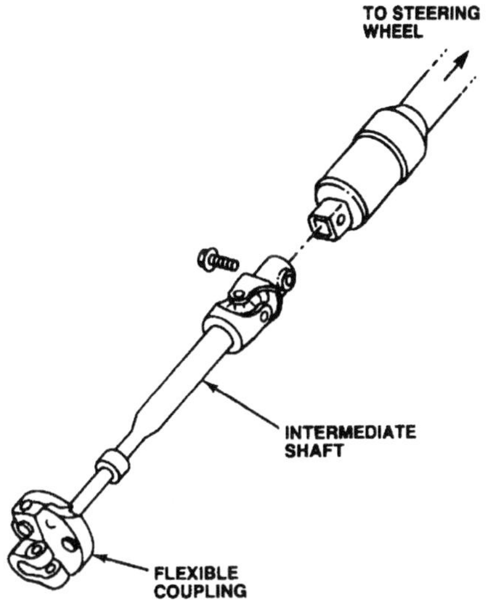

TO STEERING WHEEL

INTERMEDIATE SHAFT

FLEXIBLE COUPLING

Rack and Pinion Worm Bearing Adjustment

Meets NATEF Task: (A4-B-7) Adjust Rack and Power Worm Bearing Preload and Sector Lash (P-3)

Name ______________________________ **Date** ____________________

Make/Model __________________________ **Year** ________ **Instructor's OK** ☐

_____ **1.** Check the service information for the specified adjustment procedures and precautions for adjusting the worm bearing preload and sector lash.

A. Recommended procedure: ______________________________

____

____

B. Precautions: ______________________________

____

____

_____ **2.** Check the recommended method used to adjust the rack preload (pinion torque).

____ Shims (remove shims to increase torque, add shims to reduce torque)

____ Adjuster plug (usually tighten and loosen 60° to achieve proper torque)

____ Other (describe) ______________________________

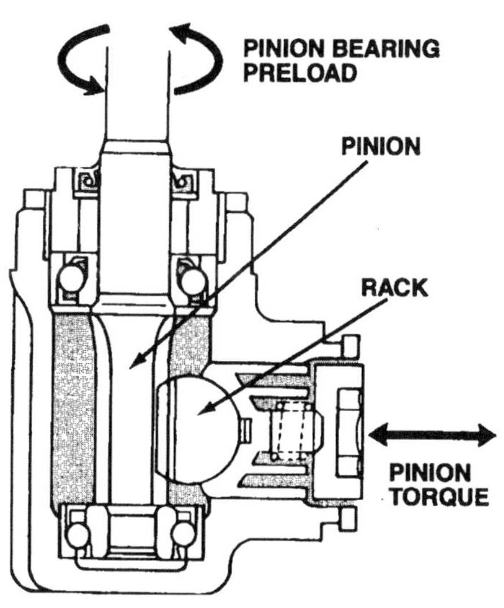

Rack and Pinion Steering Gear

Meets NATEF Task: (A4-B-8) Remove and Replace Rack and Pinion Steering Gear; Inspect Mounting Bushings and Brackets (P-1)

Name ______________________ **Date** ______________

Make/Model ______________________ **Year** ________ **Instructor's OK** ☐

_____ **1.** Check the service information and write the specified procedure to follow when removing and replacing the rack and pinion steering gear.

____

____

____

____

____

_____ **2.** The following steps are usually specified by the vehicle manufacturer.

A. Hoist the vehicle safely.

B. Disable supplemental restraint system (SRS)

C. Remove both front wheel assemblies.

D. Disconnect both outer tie rods.

E. Disconnect the intermediate shaft from the stub shaft of the rack and pinion steering gear.

F. Disconnect the power steering lines from the gear assembly (if equipped with power steering).

G. Remove the mounting brackets and remove the rack and pinion steering gear from underneath the vehicle.

_____ **3.** Carefully inspect the rubber bushings and brackets for wear or damage.

OK ____ **NOT OK** ____

_____ **4.** Show the instructor the removed rack and pinion steering gear assembly.

Instructor's OK ______________

_____ **4.** Reinstall the rack and pinion steering gear in the reverse order of disassembly.

Inner Tie Rod Ends and Bellows Boots

Meets NATEF Task: (A4-B-9) Inspect and Replace Rack and Pinion Steering Gear Inner Tie Ends (Sockets) and Bellows Boots (P-1)

Name ______________________ **Date** ______________

Make/Model ______________________ **Year** ________ **Instructor's OK** ☐

_____ **1.** Check the service information and write the specified procedure to inspect and replace the inner tie rod ends.

____

____

____

____

_____ **2.** Hoist the vehicle safely and visually check the condition of the inner tie rod end bellows boots.

____ OK
____ Cracked in places, but not all the way through (recommend replacement)
____ Cracked open places (requires replacement)
____ Missing

_____ **3.** Most vehicle manufacturers recommend that the entire rack and pinion steering gear assembly be removed from the vehicle when replacing the inner tie rod ends (ball socket assemblies).

___ **Yes** (recommend that rack be removed)
___ **No** (the tie rod end can be removed with the rack in the vehicle)

_____ **4.** Describe the method used to retain the inner ball sockets to the ends of the rack.

____ Pin
____ Rivet
____ Stacked
____ Other (describe) ______________________

_____ **5.** List all precautions found in the service information regarding this procedure.

____

_____ **6.** Describe any problems ______________________

____

Power Steering Fluid Inspection

Meets NATEF Task: (A4-B-10) Inspect Power Steering Fluid Level and Condition (P-1)

Name ______________________ **Date** ______________

Make/Model ______________________ **Year** ________ **Instructor's OK** ☐

_____ **1.** Check the service information and determine the specified type of fluid that should be used in the power steering system.

____ Power steering fluid
____ Dexron III ATF
____ Type F ATF
____ Other (specify) ______________________

_____ **2.** List any cautions or warnings as specified by the vehicle manufacturer.

____

_____ **3.** With the engine off, raise the hood and locate the power steering fluid reservoir. Describe the location: ______________________

_____ **4.** Check the level of the power steering fluid.

____ OK (at the full mark that corresponds to the temperature of the fluid)
____ Overfilled
____ Underfilled
____ Empty

_____ **5.** Check the fluid for aeration (foaming), or contamination.

____ OK (like new)
____ Darker than new, but not aerated or contaminated
____ Silver color indicating contaminated with aluminum or other metal particles from the power steering system
____ Black and thick or smells rancid
____ Other (describe) ______________________

_____ **6.** What actions are necessary? ______________________

____

____

____

Flush, Fill, and Bleed Power Steering

Meets NATEF Task: (A4-B-11) Flush, Fill, and Bleed Power Steering Systems (P-2)

Name ________________________________ **Date** ________________________

Make/Model _________________________ **Year** ________ **Instructor's OK** [ ]

A power steering system that has air trapped in the system will cause a loud, whining noise. Use the following procedure to remove any air that could have been trapped in the system during a repair procedure.

_____ **1.** Use a jack and safety stand or a lift and hoist the front wheels off the ground about one foot (30 cm).

_____ **2.** Remove the cap from the power steering reservoir and rotate the steering wheel all the way one direction, then all the way the other direction with the engine off.

> **NOTE:** As the steering wheel is being rotated, the fluid will be circulated through the system and the air will escape from the pump reservoir.

_____ **3.** Add power steering fluid as needed to keep the reservoir filled.

_____ **4.** Lower the vehicle and start the engine. Check for proper, quiet power steering gear operation.

OK _____ **NOT OK** _____

_____ **5.** If not OK, repeat the procedure again.

_____ **6.** After bleeding the system, fill the power steering reservoir to the proper level.

_____ **7.** Carefully test drive the vehicle checking for proper operation of the power steering before returning the vehicle to the customer.

Diagnose Power Steering Fluid Leakage

Meets NATEF Task: (A4-B-12) Diagnose Power Steering Fluid Leakage; Determine Necessary Action (P-2)

Name ______________________________ **Date** ______________________

Make/Model ________________________ **Year** ________ **Instructor's OK** ☐

_____ **1.** Check the service information for the specified power steering fluid.

____ Power steering fluid

____ Dexron III ATF

____ Type F ATF

____ Other (specify) ________________________________

_____ **2.** Perform a visual inspection of the power steering system and determine the location of any leaks. Hoist the vehicle if necessary. Check each area listed below that is found to be leaking.

____ Pump shaft seal area

____ Reservoir cap

____ Reservoir

____ High-pressure line at the pump

____ High-pressure line between the pump and the gear

____ High-pressure line at the gear

____ Steering gear leak near the stub shaft

____ Steering gear leak at the inner tie rod end boots

____ Low-pressure hose leak (describe the location) ________________

____ Other (describe) ________________________________

____ **3.** What action is necessary to correct the leak(s)? ________________________

____

____

____

Remove/Replace Power Steering Pump Belt

Meets NATEF Task: (A4-B-13) Remove, Inspect, Replace, and Adjust Power Steering Pump Belt (P-1)

Name ______________________________ **Date** ______________________

Make/Model ________________________ **Year** _______ **Instructor's OK** ☐

The proper operation of the power steering, as well as the air conditioning and charging system, depends on the accessory drive belt(s) being in good condition and properly tensioned.

_____ **1.** Raise the hood and carefully inspect the accessory drive belt(s).

CAUTION: Be sure the engine is off and pocket the ignition key to prevent the possibility that someone else could start the engine while you are inspecting the belt(s).

_____ **2.** Record the number and type of accessory drive belts.

____ V-belt type
____ Flat serpentine (multigroove) type

_____ **3.** Locate and record the vehicle manufacturer's specified belt tension and the actual tension for each belt:

specification:____________________ actual:______________________

NOTE: If a belt tensioner gauge is not available, press down on the belt between the pulleys with moderate force. Most vehicle manufacturers specify the deflection (movement) should be less than 1/2" (13 mm).

OK _____ **NOT OK** _____

_____ **5.** Check the tensioner for the tension mark location. Is it within the specified range according to the vehicle manufacturer's specifications?

OK _____ **NOT OK** _____

_____ **6.** Check the condition of the belt(s).

_____ OK (like new)
_____ Glazed (shiny) may need replacement if it is slipping or noisy
_____ Cracked - may need replacement if more than three cracks are in any 3 inch length per rib of the belt. **OK** _____ **NOT OK** ___

Remove/Replace Power Steering Pump

Meets NATEF Task: (A4-B-14) Remove and Reinstall Power Steering Pump (P-3)

Name ______________________________ **Date** ____________________

Make/Model __________________________ **Year** ________ **Instructor's OK** ☐

_____ **1.** Check the service information and write the specified procedure to follow for removing and reinstalling the power steering pump assembly.

____

____

____

_____ **2.** List all precautions as stated in the service information. ____________________

____

_____ **3.** Most removal and replacement procedures involve the following steps:

A. Remove the drive belt
B. Disconnect the high-pressure and low-pressure hoses at the pump.

CAUTION: Dispose of the old power steering fluid according to federal, state, and local regulations.

C. Remove the attaching bolts/nuts and remove the power steering pump assembly from the vehicle.
D. Reinstall the replacement pump assembly in the reverse order of removal.
E. Add the specified power steering fluid

_____ **4.** Raise the front wheels of the vehicle off the ground and bleed the trapped air from the power steering system by rotating the steering wheel full left and full right several times.

_____ **5.** Lower the vehicle and verify proper power steering operation.

Power Steering Pump Pulley

Meets NATEF Task: (A4-B-15) Remove and Reinstall Power Steering Pump Pulley; Check Pulley and Belt Alignment (P-3)

Name ______________________________ **Date** ______________________

Make/Model ________________________ **Year** ________ **Instructor's OK** ☐

_____ **1.** Check the service information for the specified power steering pump pulley removal and installation procedure.

____

____

_____ **2.** What special tools are needed? _______________________________

____

_____ **3.** Most specified procedures include the following steps:

A. Remove the power steering drive belt

B. Use a puller to remove the pulley

C. Use an installation tool to install the pulley on the shaft

D. Reinstall the drive belt and check for proper alignment

E. Start the engine and check for proper operation

OK ____ **NOT OK** ____

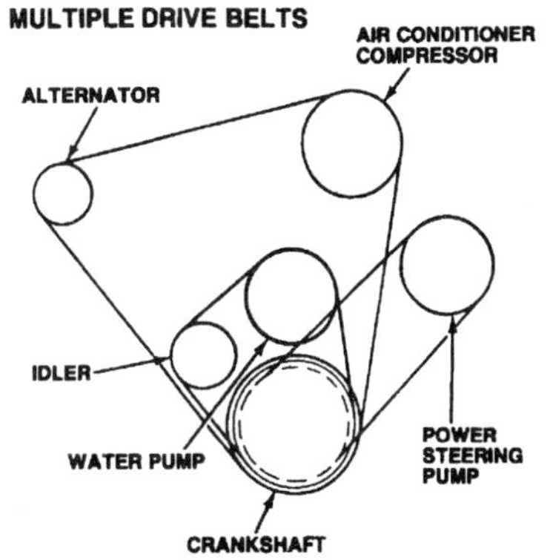

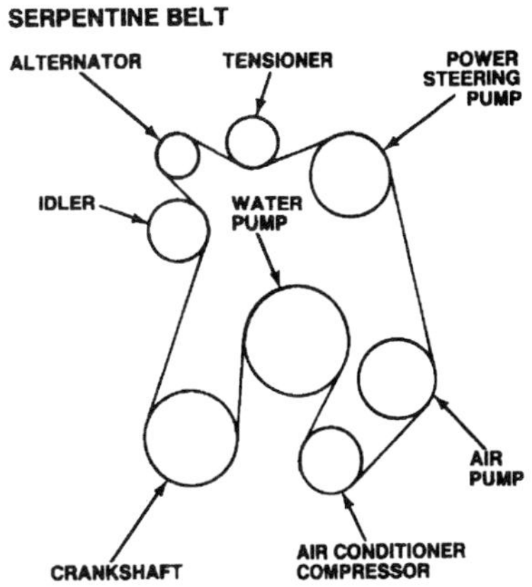

Inspect Power Steering Hoses and Fittings

Meets NATEF Task: (A4-B-16) Inspect and Replace Power Steering Hoses and Fittings (P-2)

Name ______________________ **Date** ______________

Make/Model ______________________ **Year** ________ **Instructor's OK** ☐

_____ **1.** Check the service information for the specified procedures, precautions, and torque specifications.

A. Specified procedure: ______________________

____

B. Specified precautions: ______________________

____

C. Specified torque specifications ______________

____

_____ **2.** Check the reason why the hoses and/or fittings are being replaced.

____ Leaking

____ Worn outside cover

____ Possible restriction as determined by testing

____ Recommended when replacing pump or gear assembly

____ Other (specify) ______________________

____

_____ **3.** Which hose(s) or fitting(s) was replaced?

____ High-pressure hose and fitting

____ Low-pressure hose and fitting

____ Other (specify) ______________________

____

Inspect and Replace Steering Components

Meets NATEF Task: (A4-B-17) Inspect and Replace Pitman Arm, Centerlink, Idler Arm and Steering Linkage Damper (P-2)

Name ______________________ **Date** ______________________

Make/Model ______________________ **Year** ________ **Instructor's OK** ☐

_____ **1.** Check the service information for the specified testing and inspection procedures and specifications.

A. Specified testing procedures: ______________________

____

B. Specifications: ______________________

____

_____ **2.** Check the steering components listed and note their condition.

Idler arm: ______________________

____

Pitman arm: ______________________

____

Centerlink: ______________________

____

Steering linkage damper: ______________________

____

_____ **3.** State the specified replacement procedure and list any specific tools needed.

Idler arm: Procedure ______________________

Tools ______________________

Pitman arm: Procedure ______________________

Tools ______________________

Centerlink: Procedure ______________________

Tools ______________________

Steering linkage damper: Procedure ______________________

Tools ______________________

Tie-Rod End Inspection and Replacement

Meets NATEF Task: (A4-B-18) Inspect, Replace, and Adjust Tie Rod Ends (Sockets), Tie Rod Sleeves and Clamps (P-1)

Name ________________________________ **Date** ________________________

Make/Model ________________________ **Year** ________ **Instructor's OK** [ ]

_____ **1.** Verify that the tie-rod end(s) requires replacement. Check all that apply.

_____ Torn grease boot
_____ Joint has side-to-side movement
_____ Physically damaged
_____ Other (specify) ____

_____ **2.** Hoist the vehicle safely.

_____ **3.** Compare the replacement tie-rod end with the original to be sure that the new end is correct.

_____ **4.** Remove the retaining nut and use a tie-rod puller to separate the tie-rod end from the steering knuckle and/or center link.

HINT: Often a hammer can be used to jar loose the tie-rod end especially if a downward force is exerted on the tie-rod while an assistant taps on the steering knuckle at the tie-rod end.

_____ **5.** Measure the distance between the center of the tie-rod end and the adjusting sleeve and record this distance so the replacement tie-rod end can be installed in approximately the same location so that the wheel alignment (toe setting) will be close to being correct.

_____ **6.** Unscrew the old tie-rod end and discard.

_____ **7.** Install the replacement tie-rod end and adjust to the same distance as measured and recorded in #5.

_____ **8.** Install the tie-rod end onto the steering knuckle and torque the retaining nut to factory specifications.

Torque specifications for the tie-rod retaining nut = ___________

_____ **9.** Lower the vehicle and align the vehicle before returning it to the customer.

Electronically Controlled Steering Systems

Meets NATEF Task: (A4-B-19) Test and Diagnose Components of Electronically Controlled Steering Systems Using a Scan Tool; Determine Necessary Action (P-3)

Name ______________________________ **Date** ______________________

Make/Model ________________________ **Year** ________ **Instructor's OK** ☐

_____ **1.** Check the service information for the exact testing procedure to follow when diagnosing an electronically controlled steering system.

Specified procedure: ______________________________________

____

Specified scan tool or special tool: ____________________________

____

_____ **2.** What scan tool was used? ______________________________

_____ **3.** Could the control valve or solenoid be operated by the scan tool?

Yes ____ **No** ____

_____ **4.** What method(s) is specified to test the system if a scan tool is not available?

____

_____ **5.** The system being checked is: **OK** ____ **NOT OK** ____

_____ **6.** If not OK, what action will be needed to correct the fault?

____

____

Diagnose SLA Suspension Concerns

Meets NATEF Task: (A4-C-1.1) Diagnose Short and Long Arm Suspension System Noises, Body Sway, and Uneven Riding Height Concerns; Determine Necessary Action (P-1)

Name ______________________ **Date** ______________

Make/Model ____________________ **Year** ________ **Instructor's OK** ☐

_____ **1.** State the customer concerns:

____

____

____

____

____

_____ **2.** Perform a visual inspection of the vehicle including the following:

A. **Ride height** Equal front and rear? **OK** ____ **NOT OK** ____

B. **Ride height** Left and right? **OK** ____ **NOT OK** ____

C. **Tires** Size and condition **OK** ____ **NOT OK** ____

Describe: _______________________________

D. **Front wheel alignment** look OK? **OK** ____ **NOT OK** ____

Describe any faults: _______________________________

_____ **3.** Test drive the vehicle and note any faults with the vehicle handling.

____ OK

____ Sways while cornering or turning

____ Noise from suspension (describe when and type of noise) ______________

____

____ Other (describe) _______________________________

____ **4.** Check for any technical service bulletins (TSBs) that are suspension related.

____

____

Diagnose Strut Suspension Concerns

Meets NATEF Task: (A4-C-1.2) Diagnose Strut Suspension Noises, Body Sway, and Uneven Riding Height Concerns; Determine Necessary Action (P-1)

Name ______________________ **Date** ______________________

Make/Model ______________________ **Year** ________ **Instructor's OK** ☐

_____ **1.** State the customer concerns:

____

____

____

_____ **2.** Perform a visual inspection of the vehicle including the following:

A. **Ride height** Equal front and rear? **OK** ____ **NOT OK** ____

B. **Ride height** Left and right? **OK** ____ **NOT OK** ____

C. **Tires** Size and condition **OK** ____ **NOT OK** ____

Describe: ____

D. **Front wheel alignment** look OK? **OK** ____ **NOT OK** ____

Describe any faults: ____

_____ **3.** Test drive the vehicle and note any faults with the vehicle handling.

____ OK
____ Sways while cornering or turning
____ Noise from suspension (describe when and type of noise) ______________

____

____ Other (describe) ____

____ **4.** Check for any technical service bulletins (TSBs) that are suspension related.

____

____

Suspension Identification

Meets NATEF Task: (A4-A-1) Identify and Interpret Suspension Concerns; Determine Necessary Action (P-1)

Name ______________________________ **Date** ______________________

Make/Model ________________________ **Year** ________ **Instructor's OK** ☐

_____ **1.** Identify the type of front suspension. ______________________________

_____ **2.** Locate and inspect the condition of the control arm bushings.

OK ___ **NOT OK** ___

_____ **3.** Locate all ball-joints. Location = ______________________________

_____ **4.** Is the vehicle equipped with strut rods?

Yes ____ **No** ____

_____ **5.** Is the vehicle equipped with a stabilizer bar?

Front - **Yes** ____ **No** ____

Rear - **Yes** ____ **No** ____

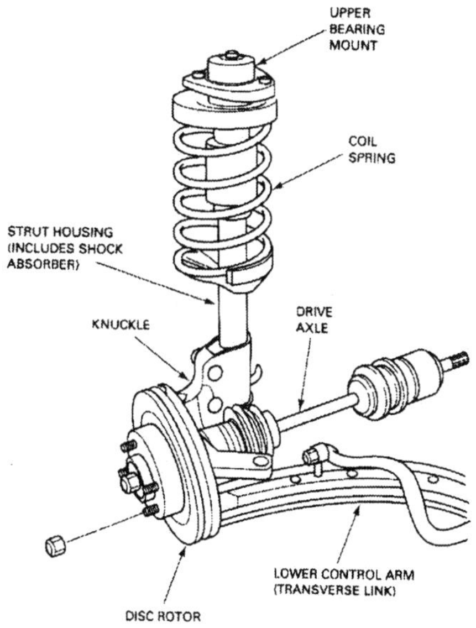

_____ **6.** Locate and inspect the stabilizer links and bushings. **OK** ____ **NOT OK** ____

_____ **7.** Locate and determine the condition of the shock absorbers. **OK** ____ **NOT OK** ____

_____ **8.** Identify the type of rear suspension. ______________________________

Remove/Install Control Arm Components

Meets NATEF Task: (A4-C-1.3) Remove, Inspect, and Install Upper and Lower Control Arms, Bushings, Shafts, and Rebound Bumpers (P-3)

Name ______________________________ **Date** ____________________

Make/Model ________________________ **Year** ________ **Instructor's OK** ☐

_____ **1.** Check the service information and determine the specified procedures to remove and install control arm bushings and related components.

____
____
____
____
____
____

_____ **2.** Check the service information and determine the specified special tools needed to replace control arm bushings.

Tool part # ____________ Description ______________________

Tool part # ____________ Description ______________________

Tool part # ____________ Description ______________________

Tool part # ____________ Description ______________________

_____ **3.** Inspect the rebound bumpers (describe the location): ____________________

____

____ OK (like new)

____ Worn or damaged (describe location and fault) ____________________

____

____ Missing (describe location) ______________________

_____ **4.** Based on a visual inspection, what action is necessary? ____________________

____

Strut Rod Bushings

Meets NATEF Task: (A4-C-1.4) Remove, Inspect, and Install Strut Rods (Compression/Tension Rods) and Bushings (P-2)

Name ______________________ **Date** ______________

Make/Model ______________________ **Year** ________ **Instructor's OK** [ ]

_____ **1.** Which of the following symptoms are present requiring the replacement of the strut? rod bushings?

____ Pull to one side during braking only
____ Noise while driving
____ Noise (clunk) during braking
____ Other (describe) ______________________

_____ **2.** Check the location of the strut rod bushing.

____ Forward of the front wheels
____ Rearward of the front wheels

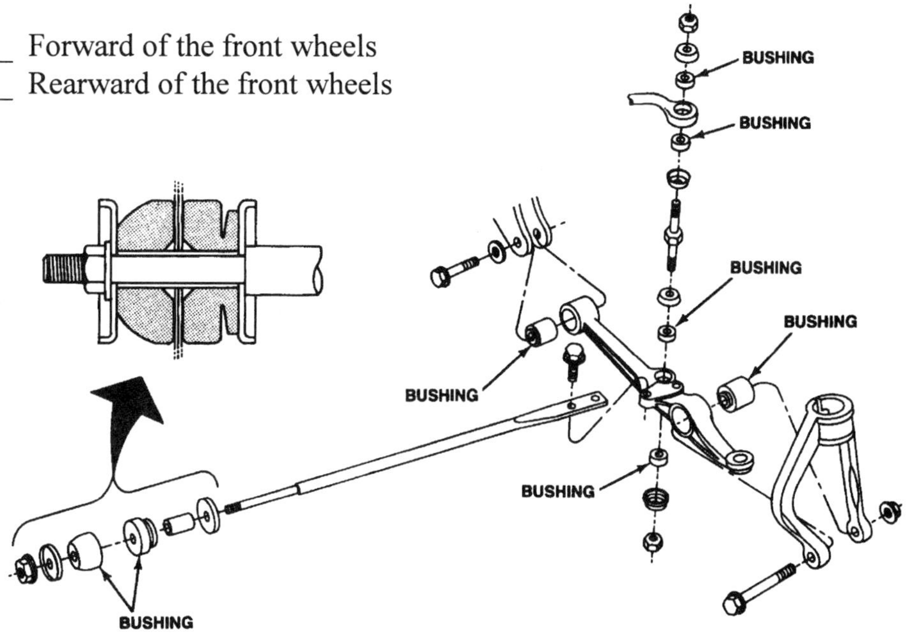

_____ **3.** Check the service information to determine the specified procedure for replacing strut rod bushings.

____

____

_____ **4.** List the special tools needed. ______________________

Ball-Joint Testing

Meets NATEF Task: (A4-C-1.1) Diagnose SLA Suspension System Noises, Body Sway and Uneven Riding Height Concerns; Determine Necessary Action (P-1)

Name ______________________________ **Date** ____________________

Make/Model ________________________ **Year** ________ **Instructor's OK** ☐

_____ **1.** Determine the load-carrying ball-joint.

_____ upper _____ lower _____ both

_____ **2.** Is this a wear indicator ball-joint? _____ **Yes** _____ **No** If yes, observe the area around the grease fitting with the vehicle weight on the ground.

A. Is it flush with the rest of the bottom of the joint? _____ **Yes** _____ **No**

B. Is it loose? _____ **Yes** _____ **No**

_____ **3.** Position the floor jack correctly for testing. Describe: ______________________

____

_____ **4.** Locate and record the specification for axial play:

load-carrying = ______________ follower = ______________

_____ **5.** Locate and record the specification for lateral play:

load-carrying = ______________ follower = ______________

_____ **6.** Test both load-carrying and follower ball joints on both the left and the right side and record your results.

	Left	**Right**
Load-Carrying	______	______
Follower	______	______

OK ____ **NOT OK** ____

Ball-Joint Replacement

Meets NATEF Task: (A4-C-1.5) Remove, Inspect and Install Upper and/or Lower Ball Joints (P-2)

Name ______________________________ **Date** ______________________

Make/Model __________________________ **Year** ________ **Instructor's OK** ☐

_____ **1.** Check the service information and determine the specified ball-joint replacement procedure. ____
____

_____ **2.** What special tools are needed? ______________________________

_____ **3.** A commonly recommended procedure includes:

____ Hoist the vehicle safely.

____ Remove the wheel/tire assembly.

____ Remove the cotter key retaining the ball-joint stud nut.

____ Remove the ball-joint stud nut.

____ Separate the ball-joint from the control arm (or knuckle) following the service information procedure and tool(s).

____ Using a C-clamp-shaped tool with the proper adapter, press the ball-joint from the control arm.

_____ **4.** Show the instructor the removed ball-joint.

Instructor's OK ____________________

_____ **5.** Replace the ball-joint using the proper adapters.

_____ **6.** Reinstall the control arm (or knuckle) and reattach the ball-joint. Install the ball-joint stud nut and torque to specifications. Specifications = _____ lb.-ft.

_____ **7.** Install a new cotter key.

NOTE: The vehicle wheels should be aligned after replacing the ball-joints.

Steering Knuckle Diagnosis

Meets NATEF Task: (A4-C-1.6) Remove, Inspect, and Install Steering Knuckle Assemblies (P-3)

Name ______________________________ **Date** ______________________

Make/Model __________________________ **Year** ________ **Instructor's OK** ☐

_____ **1.** Check the service information for the specified procedure to follow to determine if the steering knuckle is damaged or bent.

____

____

____

The distance between the rotor and the steering knuckle should be the same on both sides of the vehicle. Dimension "A" checks if the steering arm is bent, and dimension "B" checks if the spindle is bent.

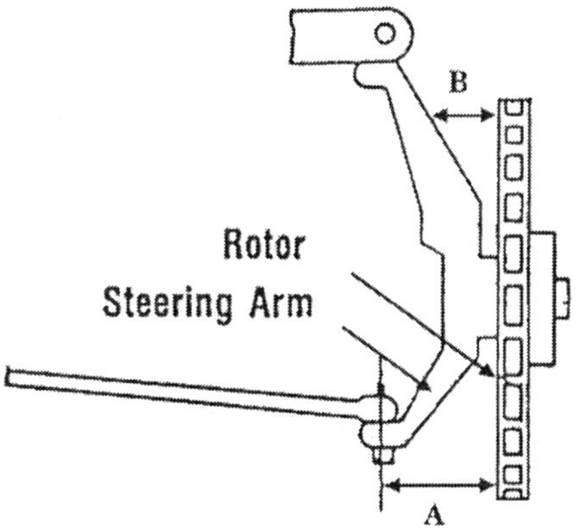

_____ **2.** Because the steering arm and the steering knuckle are often an integral part, determine the specified toe out on turn (TOOT).

Outside wheel = _________ Inside wheel = _________

_____ **3.** Measure the left and right side toe out on turns.

Left = __________ Right = __________

_____ **4.** Based on the inspection, what action is needed? ______________________________

____

Steering Knuckle Replacement

Meets NATEF Task: (A4-C-1.6) Remove, Inspect, and Install Steering Knuckle Assemblies (P-3)

Name ______________________________ **Date** ______________________

Make/Model ___________________________ **Year** ________ **Instructor's OK** ☐

_____ **1.** Check the service information and determine the specified procedure.

____

____

_____ **2.** List the tools needed. ___________________________________

____

_____ **3.** Show the instructor the removed steering knuckle. **Instructor's OK** __________

_____ **4.** List the torque specifications for all fasteners. ______________________

____

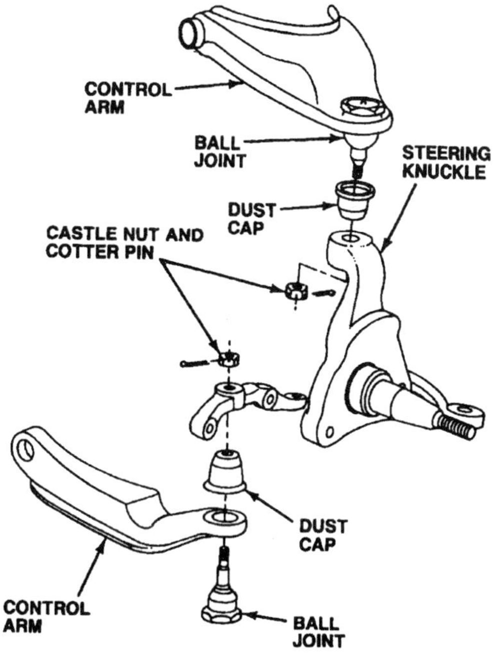

_____ **5.** After replacing the steering knuckle assembly, the wheel alignment should be checked and corrected.

Coil Spring Replacement

Meets NATEF Task: (A4-C-1.7) Remove, Inspect, and Install Short and Long Arm Suspension Systems, Coil Springs, and Spring Insulators (P-2)

Name ______________________ **Date** ______________________

Make/Model ______________________ **Year** ________ **Instructor's OK** ☐

_____ **1.** Check the service information and determine the specified procedure for removing and installing front coil springs.

____

____

____

____

_____ **2.** List the tools needed.

____

____

____

____

____

_____ **3.** List all precautions stated in the service information.

____

____

_____ **4.** Show the instructor the removed spring(s).

Instructor's OK ______________

_____ **5.** List the torque specifications for the fasteners.

____

____

____

COIL SPRING

Torsion Bar

Meets NATEF Task: (A4-C-1.8) Remove, Inspect, Install, and Adjust Suspension System Torsion Bars; Inspect Mounts (P-3)

Name ______________________ **Date** ______________

Make/Model ____________________ **Year** ________ **Instructor's OK** [ ]

_____ **1.** Check the service information for the specified removal and reinstallation procedure.

____

____

____

____

_____ **2.** List the tools needed.

____

____

____

____

____

_____ **3.** Check the service information and describe the proper ride height adjustment procedure.

____

____

____

____

____

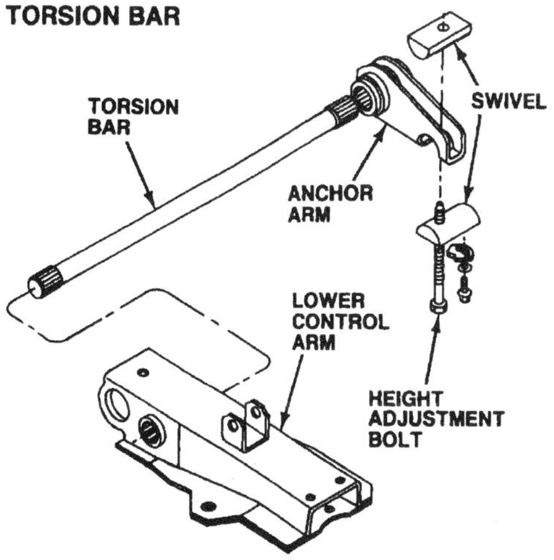

TORSION BAR

TORSION BAR

SWIVEL

ANCHOR ARM

LOWER CONTROL ARM

HEIGHT ADJUSTMENT BOLT

_____ **4.** Inspect the torsion bar mounts.

OK ___ **NOT OK** ___

Describe the faults and needed action.

____

____

Stabilizer Bar Bushings

Meets NATEF Task: (A4-C-1.9) Remove, Inspect, and Install Stabilizer Bar Bushings, Brackets, and Links (P-2)

Name ______________________ **Date** ______________________

Make/Model ______________________ **Year** ________ **Instructor's OK** ☐

_____ **1.** Check the service information and determine the specified procedure for replacing stabilizer bar bushings.

____

____

NOTE: Most vehicle manufacturers recommend that the bushings on both sides of the vehicle be replaced even if the bushings on only one side are worn or damaged.

_____ **2.** List any special tools needed. ____

____

_____ **3.** List the torque specifications for the fasteners. ______________________________

____

_____ **4.** Check the brackets and links. **OK** ____ **NOT OK** ____

If not OK, describe the condition and the action needed. ______________________

____

____

MacPherson Strut Service

Meets NATEF Task: (A4-C-1.10) Remove, Inspect, and Install Strut Cartridge or Assembly, Strut Coil Spring, Insulators (Silencers), and Upper Strut Bearing Mount (P-1)

Name ______________________ **Date** ______________________

Make/Model ______________________ **Year** ________ **Instructor's OK** ☐

_____ **1.** Check the service information for the specified service procedure.

____

____

____

_____ **2.** Safely support the vehicle on jacks and/or the lift.

_____ **3.** Remove the upper and lower attaching bolts and nuts.

_____ **4.** Carefully remove the MacPherson strut assembly from the vehicle.

_____ **5.** Compress the coil spring with the proper equipment and replace the strut assembly.

Show the instructor the disassembled unit.

Instructor's OK ________

_____ **6.** Reinstall the complete assembly.

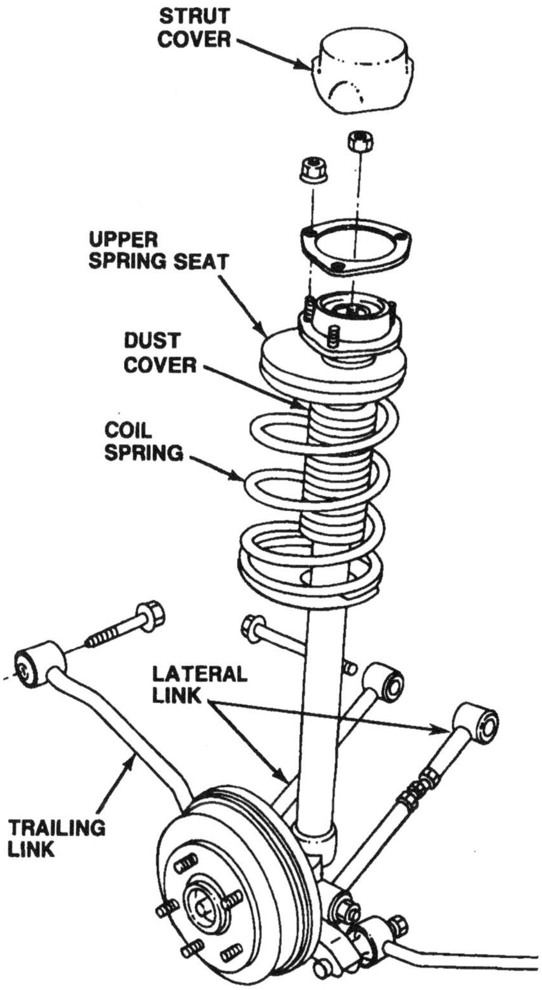

NOTE: The vehicle should be aligned after replacing the strut assembly.

Suspension and Steering Lubrication

Meets NATEF Task: (A4-C-1.11) Lubricate Suspension and Steering System (P-2)

Name ______________________________ **Date** ______________________

Make/Model ________________________ **Year** ________ **Instructor's OK** ☐

_____ **1.** Check the service information regarding lubrication points. Describe the location.

____

____

_____ **2.** What is the specified grease or lubricant? ______________________

____

_____ **3.** How many sealed ball and socket joints are there that do not require lubrication?

____

Rear Coil Springs

Meets NATEF Task: (A4-C-2.1) Remove, Inspect, and Install Coil Springs and Spring Insulators (P-2)

Name ______________________________ **Date** ______________________

Make/Model ________________________ **Year** ________ **Instructor's OK** ☐

_____ **1.** Check the service information for the specified rear coil spring removal and installation procedure.

____

____

____

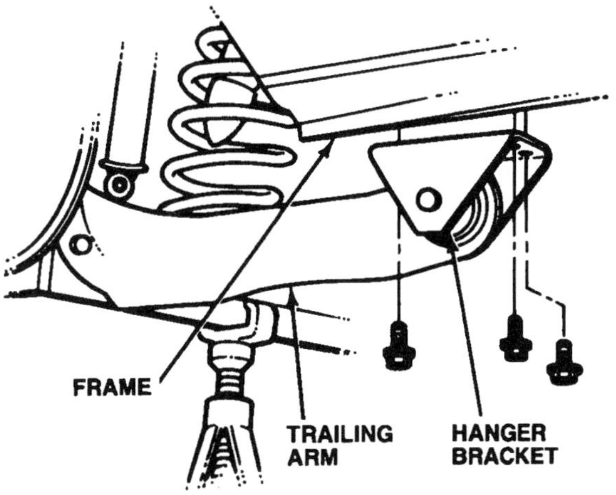

FRAME

TRAILING ARM

HANGER BRACKET

_____ **2.** List the tools and equipment needed as specified by the vehicle manufacturer.

____

____

____

_____ **3.** Show the instructor the removed coil spring(s). **Instructor's OK** ____________

_____ **4.** List all safety precautions. ______________________________

____

_____ **5.** List the torque specifications for all fasteners. ______________________

____

Transverse Suspension Links

Meets NATEF Task: (A4-C-2.2) Remove, Inspect, and Install Transverse Links, Control Arms, Bushings, and Mounts (P-2)

Name ______________________________ **Date** ____________________

Make/Model ____________________________ **Year** ________ **Instructor's OK** [ ]

_____ **1.** Check the service information for the specified procedure to remove and replace transverse (lateral) links, bushings, and mounts.

____

____

____

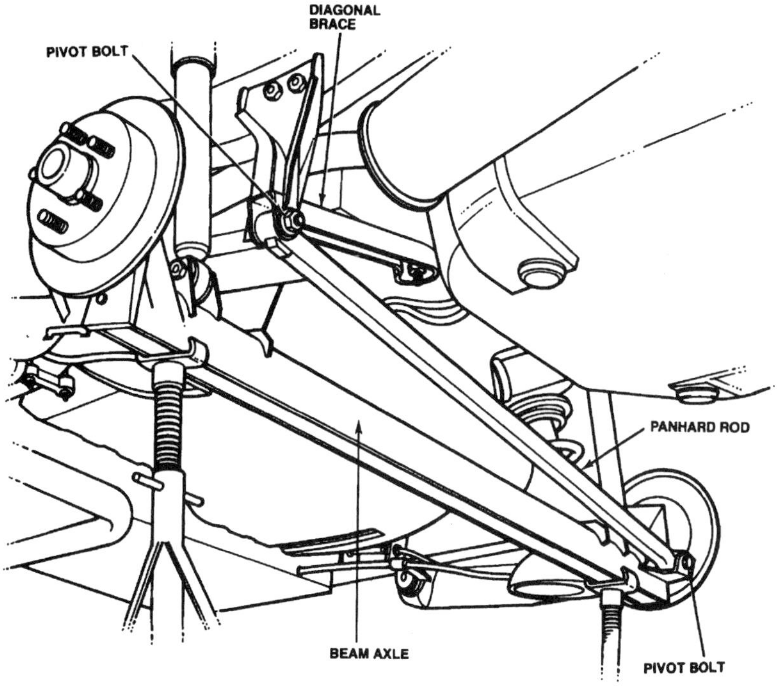

_____ **2.** List the tools and equipment needed. ______________________________

____

_____ **3.** Show the instructor the removed transverse link. **Instructor's OK** __________

_____ **4.** List the tightening torque specifications for the affected fasteners. __________

____

Rear Leaf Springs

Meets NATEF Task: (A4-C-2.3) Remove, Inspect, and Install Leaf Springs, Leaf Spring Insulators (silencers), Shackles, Brackets, Bushings, and Mounts (P-3)

Name ______________________________ **Date** ______________________

Make/Model ___________________________ **Year** ________ **Instructor's OK** ☐

_____ **1.** Check the service information for the specified procedure for the removal and reinstallation of rear leaf springs.

____

____

____

_____ **2.** List the tools and equipment needed. ______________________________

____

_____ **3.** Show the instructor the removed rear leaf spring(s). **Instructor's OK** __________

_____ **4.** List the tightening torque specifications for the affected fasteners. _____________

____

Rear Strut Replacement

Meets NATEF Task: (A4-C-2.4) Remove, Inspect, and Install Strut Cartridge or Assembly, Strut Coil Spring, and Insulators (Silencers) (P-2)

Name ______________________________ **Date** ______________________

Make/Model ________________________ **Year** ________ **Instructor's OK** ☐

_____ **1.** Check the service information for the specified procedure for the removal and reinstallation of rear struts.

____

____

____

_____ **2.** List the tools and equipment needed. ______________________

____

____

____

_____ **3.** Show the instructor the removed rear strut.

Instructor's OK ___________

_____ **4.** List the tightening torque specifications for the affected fasteners. ____________________

____

____

____

____

Front Shock Absorber Replacement

Meets NATEF Task: (A4-C-3.1) Inspect, Remove, and Replace Shock Absorbers (P-1)

Name ______________________________ **Date** ____________________

Make/Model ________________________ **Year** ________ **Instructor's OK** ☐

_____ **1.** Verify that the front shock absorber requires replacement. Check all that apply:

_____ bent or damaged shock or mounting hardware
_____ shock absorber is leaking hydraulic fluid
_____ excessively worn - causing tire wear or riding comfort problems
_____ other (specify) ________________________________

_____ **2.** Compare the replacement shocks to the original shocks to be sure that they are correct.
OK _____ **NOT OK** _____
NOTE: All shock absorbers should be replaced in pairs only. Do not replace just one shock absorber.

_____ **3.** Check the service information for the specified replacement procedure. ___________
____
____

HINT: Many shocks on rear-wheel-drive vehicles can be broken off using a deep-well socket and a long extension. By rocking the extension back and forth, the top of the shock will usually break off saving the time and effort it takes to remove a nut that is often rusted in place after many years of service.

_____ **4.** Safely hoist the vehicle.

_____ **5.** Remove the lower shock absorber retaining bolts (nuts) as per the service information instructions.
CAUTION: Be ready to catch the shock absorber because it will likely fall after removing the last retaining bolt (nut).

_____ **6.** Show the instructor the removed shock absorber. **Instructor's OK** ___________

_____ **7.** Extend the rod on the replacement shock and install the lower retaining bolts (nuts).

_____ **8.** Lower the vehicle and install the upper retaining fastener.

_____ **9.** Bounce the vehicle to check that the replacement shock does not interfere with any part of the suspension or frame.

_____ **10.** Test drive the vehicle before returning it to the customer.

Rear Shock Absorber Replacement

Meets NATEF Task: (A4-C-3.1) Inspect, Remove, and Replace Shock Absorbers (P-1)

Name ______________________________ **Date** ______________________

Make/Model __________________________ **Year** ________ **Instructor's OK** ☐

_____ **1.** Verify that the front shock absorber requires replacement. Check all that apply:

_____ bent or damaged shock or mounting hardware
_____ shock absorber is leaking hydraulic fluid
_____ excessively worn - causing tire wear or riding comfort problems
_____ other (specify) ______________________________

_____ **2.** Compare the replacement shocks to the original shocks to be sure that they are correct.
OK _____ **NOT OK** _____

NOTE: All shock absorbers should be replaced in pairs only. Do not replace just one shock absorber.

_____ **3.** Check the service information for the specified replacement procedure. ___________

____

NOTE: The upper shock mount may be located in the trunk or underneath the vehicle.

_____ **4.** Safely hoist the vehicle.

_____ **5.** Use tall safety stands to support the rear axle assembly.

_____ **6.** Remove the lower shock absorber retaining bolts (nuts).
CAUTION: Be ready to catch the shock absorber because it will likely fall after removing the last retaining bolt (nut).

_____ **7.** Show the instructor the removed shock absorber. **Instructor's OK** ____________

_____ **8.** Extend the rod on the replacement shock and install the lower retaining bolts (nuts).

_____ **9.** Lower the vehicle and install the upper retaining fastener.

_____ **10.** Bounce the vehicle to check that the replacement shock does not interfere with any part of the suspension or frame.

_____ **11.** Test drive the vehicle before returning it to the customer.

Wheel Bearing Service

Meets NATEF Task: (A4-C-3.2) Remove, Inspect, and Service or Replace Front and Rear Wheel Bearings (P-1)

Name ______________________________ **Date** ____________________

Make/Model ________________________ **Year** ________ **Instructor's OK** ☐

_____ **1.** Remove the wheel cover and the hub dust cap (grease cap).

_____ **2.** Remove and discard the cotter key.

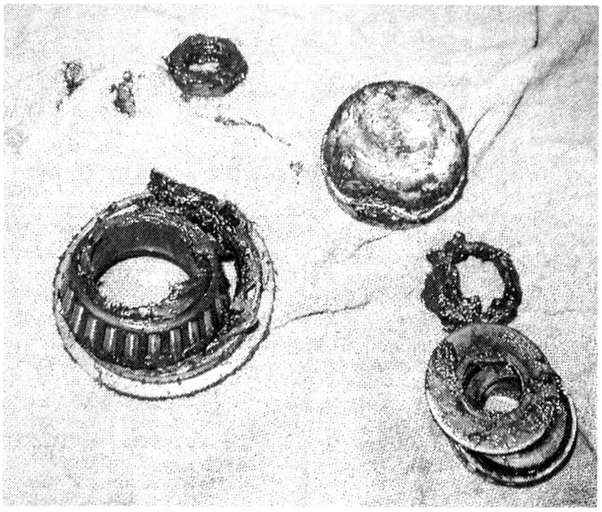

_____ **3.** Remove the spindle nut, washer and outer bearing.

_____ **4.** Remove inner and outer bearing and grease seal.

_____ **5.** Thoroughly clean the bearing in solvent and denatured alcohol or brake cleaner and blow it dry with compressed air.

_____ **6.** Closely inspect the bearing for wear or damage.

_____ **7.** Show the instructor the cleaned bearing. **Instructor's OK** ____________

_____ **8.** Repack the bearing with the correct type of wheel bearing grease.

_____ **9.** Install a new grease seal using a seal installing tool.

_____ **10.** Correctly adjust the bearing preload:

- ____ Install the spindle nut and while rotating the tire assembly, tighten (snug only, 12 to 30 lb.-ft.) with a wrench to "seat" the bearing correctly in the race.
- _____ While still rotating the tire assembly, loosen the nut approximately 1/2 turn and then *hand tighten only*.
- _____ Install a new cotter key (the common size is 1/8" diameter and 1.5 inches long).
- _____ Bend the ends of the cotter key up and around the nut to prevent interference with the dust cap.

_____ **11.** Install the hub dust cap (grease cap) and wheel cover.

Electronic Suspension Diagnosis

Meets NATEF Task: (A4-C-3.3) Test and Diagnose Components of Electronically Controlled Suspension Systems Using a Scan Tool; Determine Necessary Action (P-3)

Name ______________________________ **Date** ____________________

Make/Model __________________________ **Year** ________ **Instructor's OK** ☐

_____ **1.** Check the service information and determine the specified testing procedures.

____

____

____

_____ **2.** Check the service information and compare normal scan tool readings of the electronically controlled suspension system to the actual readings obtained from the vehicle.

Parameter	Normal Reading	Actual Reading
____________	____________	____________
____________	____________	____________
____________	____________	____________
____________	____________	____________
____________	____________	____________
____________	____________	____________
____________	____________	____________
____________	____________	____________

_____ **3.** Based on the service information and the scan tool data, what is the necessary action?

____

____

____

Steering and Suspension Concerns

Meets NATEF Task: (A4-D-1) Differentiate Between Steering and Suspension Concerns Using Principles of Steering Geometry (Caster, Camber, Toe, etc.) (P-1)

Name ______________________ **Date** ______________________

Make/Model ______________________ **Year** ________ **Instructor's OK** ☐

_____ **1.** Check the service information to determine the alignment specifications.

Camber = __________ Caster = __________ Toe = __________

_____ **2.** Hoist the vehicle on the alignment rack and install the wheel sensors.

_____ **3.** Compensate the wheel sensors.

_____ **4.** Lower the vehicle and jounce (bounce) to center the suspension.

_____ **5.** Read the rear camber and toe.

	LR	**RR**
Camber	_____	_____
Toe	_____	_____

Total rear toe = _______

_____ **6.** Read the front camber and toe.

	LF	**RF**
Camber	_____	_____
Toe	_____	_____

Total front toe = _______

_____ **7.** Perform a caster sweep to determine the front caster and SAI.

	LF	**RF**
Caster	_____	_____
SAI	_____	_____

Based on the alignment angles, what action is needed? ____________________

____

____

Vehicle Handling Diagnosis

Meets NATEF Task: (A4-D-2) Diagnose Vehicle Wander, Drift, Hard Steering, Bump Steer, Memory Steer, Torque Steer, and Steering Return Concerns; Determine Necessary Action (P-1)

Name ______________________________ **Date** ____________________

Make/Model ____________________________ **Year** ________ **Instructor's OK** ☐

_____ **1.** Test drive the vehicle and check all of the following.

OK ____ **NOT OK** ____ Wander (unstable)

OK ____ **NOT OK** ____ Drift (pulls slightly to one side)

OK ____ **NOT OK** ____ Hard steering

OK ____ **NOT OK** ____ Bump steer (The vehicle travels left or right by itself, while driving without steering wheel input. Usually caused by unlevel steering linkage.)

OK ____ **NOT OK** ____ Memory steer (The vehicle pulls to the right after a right turn and pulls to the left after a left turn. Usually caused by a defective strut upper mount or stiff ball-joints.)

OK ____ **NOT OK** ____ Torque steer (front-wheel-drive vehicle only) (accelerates rapidly) (Does the vehicle pull to one side? Often caused by unequal tire pressures or a collapsed engine or transaxle mount.)

OK ____ **NOT OK** ____ Steering wheel returnability

_____ **2.** Based on the test drive, what actions are necessary to correct the concerns?

____

____

____

____

Pre-Alignment Inspection

Meets NATEF Task: (A4-D-3) Perform Prealignment Inspection; Perform Necessary Action (P-1)

Name ______________________________ **Date** ______________________

Make/Model ______________________ **Year** ________ **Instructor's OK** ☐

_____ **1.** Check tires. Both front tires and both rear tires should be checked for the following:

A. Correct tire pressure

B. Same size and brand

C. Same tread depth

OK _____ **NOT OK** _____

_____ **2.** Perform a dry-park test to check for any looseness in the steering and suspension components such as:

A. Tie rods

B. Idler arms

C. Ball-joints

D. Control arm bushings

E. Loose or defective wheel bearings

OK _____ **NOT OK** _____

_____ **3.** Check for proper ride height.

A. Front and rear

B. Left and right

OK _____ **NOT OK** _____

Alignment Specification

Meets NATEF Task: (A4-D-1 through 14) Necessary Information Needed to Perform the Tasks Listed

Name ______________________________ **Date** ______________________

Make/Model ________________________ **Year** ________ **Instructor's OK** ☐

_____ **1.** Find the following alignment angle specifications for your vehicle:

Camber (left) preferred = _______ minimum _______ maximum _______

Camber (right) preferred = _______ minimum _______ maximum _______

Caster (left) preferred = _______ minimum _______ maximum _______

Caster (right) preferred = _______ minimum _______ maximum _______

Front toe preferred = _______ minimum _______ maximum _______

Rear camber preferred = _______ minimum _______ maximum _______

Total rear toe preferred = _______ minimum _______ maximum _______

_____ **2.** Determine the diagnostic angle specifications for your vehicle:

Toe-out on turn (TOOT) inside wheel = _______ degrees

outside wheel = _______ degrees

Maximum allowable variation = _______ degrees

Steering axis inclination (SAI) left = _______

right = _______

Maximum allowable difference = _______

Alignment Angle Readings

Meets NATEF Task: (A4-D-1 through 14) Necessary Information Needed to Perform the Tasks Listed

Name ______________________________ **Date** ______________________

Make/Model ________________________ **Year** ________ **Instructor's OK** [ ]

_____ **1.** Hoist the vehicle on the alignment rack and install the wheel sensors.

_____ **2.** Compensate the wheel sensors as per the alignment equipment manufacturer's recommended procedure.

_____ **3.** Lower the vehicle and jounce (bounce) to center the suspension.

_____ **4.** Read the rear camber and toe.

	LR	**RR**
Camber	_____	_____
Toe	_____	_____

Total rear toe = _______

_____ **5.** Read the front camber and toe.

	LF	**RF**
Camber	_____	_____
Toe	_____	_____

Total front toe = _______

_____ **6.** Perform a caster sweep to determine the front caster and SAI.

	LF	**RF**
Caster	_____	_____
SAI	_____	_____

Describe what (if anything) is wrong with the present alignment.

____

Ride Height Measurement

Meets NATEF Task: (A4-D-4) Measure Vehicle Riding Height; Determine Necessary Action (P-1)

Name ______________________________ **Date** ____________________

Make/Model ________________________ **Year** _______ **Instructor's OK** ☐

_____ **1.** Check the service information or the chart in the appendix of this worktext and determine the specified vehicle riding height.

Specification for front = ______________

Specification for rear = ______________

_____ **2.** Measure the actual vehicle riding height.

Actual front = ______________

Actual rear = ______________

OK ____ **NOT OK** ____ Describe the faults: ______________________

____

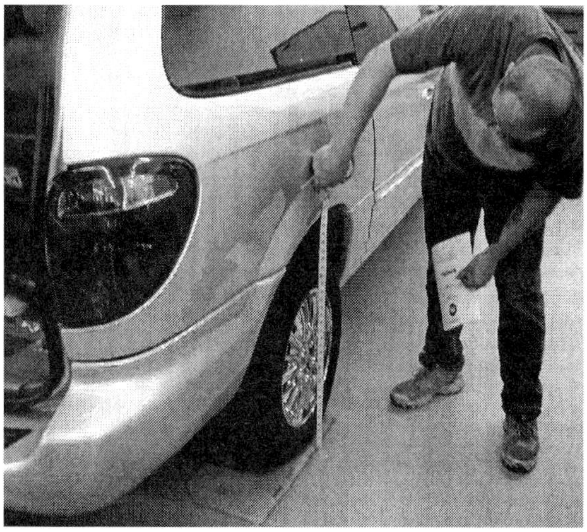

_____ **3.** What necessary action is needed to restore proper riding height? _______________

____

____

Front and Rear Camber

Meets NATEF Task: (A4-D-5) Check and Adjust Front and Rear Wheel Camber; Perform Necessary Action (P-1)

Name ______________________ **Date** ______________________

Make/Model ______________________ **Year** ________ **Instructor's OK** ☐

_____ **1.** Check with the service information and determine the specified camber angle for both front and rear wheels.

Front camber specification = __________

Rear camber specification = __________

CAMBER

+ −

POSITIVE NEGATIVE

_____ **2.** Following the alignment equipment manufacturer's recommended procedure, measure the camber angles.

	Left	**Right**
Rear camber	__________	__________
Front camber	__________	__________

_____ **3.** Check the service information to determine the specified method for changing the rear and front camber angles.

Method	**Rear Camber**	**Front Camber**
No factory adjustment provided	__________	__________
Shims	__________	__________
Eccentric cams	__________	__________
Slots	__________	__________
Other (specify) __________	__________	__________

_____ **4.** Perform the necessary camber angle adjustment to achieve specified camber angles for both front and rear wheels.

Check and Adjust Caster

Meets NATEF Task: (A4-D-6) Check and Adjust Caster; Perform Necessary Action (P-1)

Name ______________________________ **Date** ______________________

Make/Model ________________________ **Year** ________ **Instructor's OK** ☐

_____ **1.** Check the service information and determine the specified caster setting.

Caster specification = _______________

_____ **2.** Following the alignment equipment manufacturer's recommended procedure, measure the caster angles.

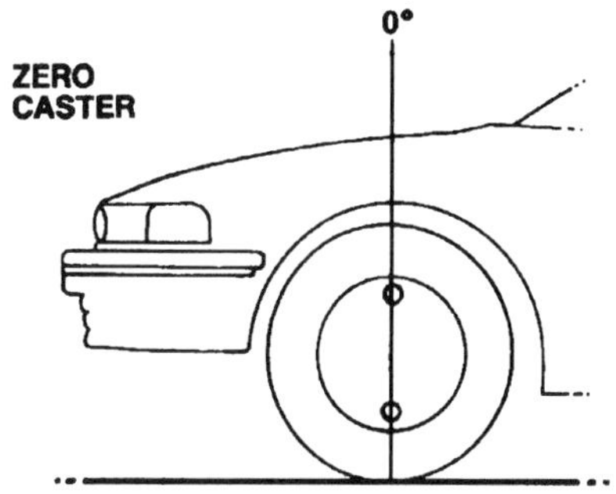

Left side actual caster angle = ___________

Right side actual caster angle = ___________

_____ **3.** Check the service information to determine the specified method for changing the caster angle(s).

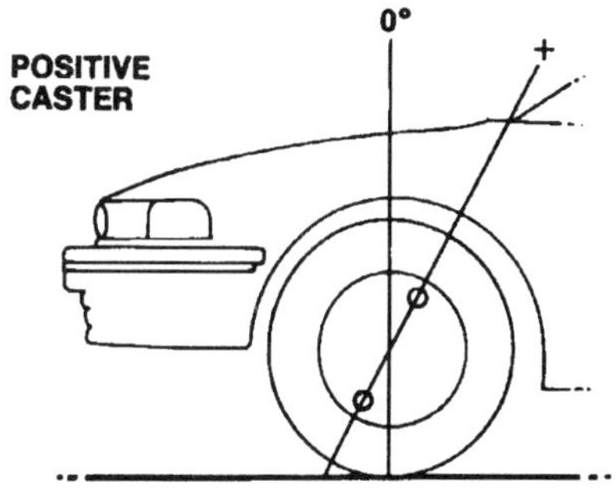

____ No factory adjustment method is provided

____ Strut rods

____ Shims

____ Eccentric cams

____ Slots

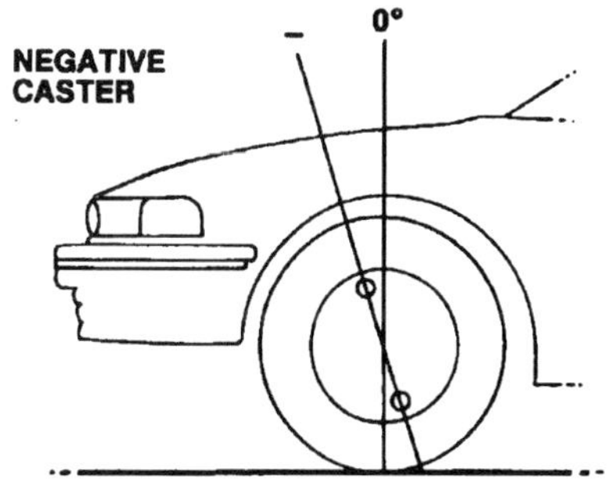

_____ **4.** Perform the necessary caster angle adjustment to achieve the specified angles on both front wheels.

Front Wheel Toe

Meets NATEF Task: (A4-D-7) Check and Adjust Front Wheel Toe; Adjust as Needed (P-1)

Name ______________________________ **Date** ____________________

Make/Model ________________________ **Year** ________ **Instructor's OK** [ ]

_____ **1.** Check the service information and determine the specified toe setting.

Front wheel toe specification = __________

_____ **2.** Following the alignment equipment manufacturer's recommended procedure, measure the front wheel toe.

Left wheel toe = __________

Right wheel toe = __________

Total toe = __________

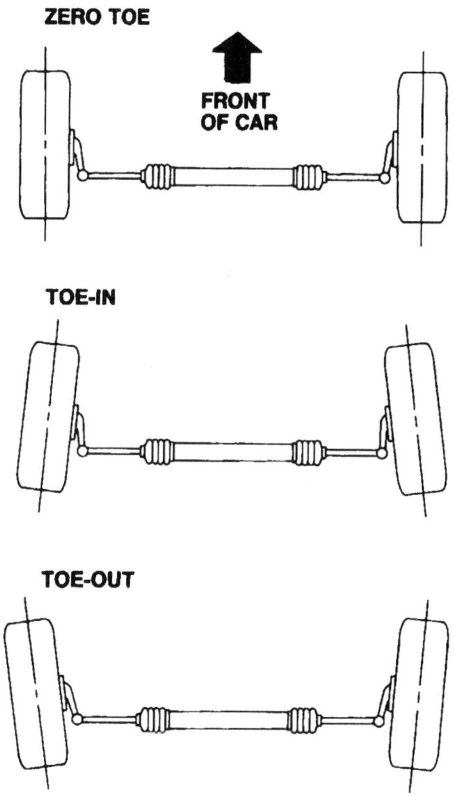

ZERO TOE

FRONT OF CAR

TOE-IN

TOE-OUT

_____ **3.** Check the service information to determine the specified method for changing front toe.

____ Tie rod sleeve (one side only provided)

____ Tie rod sleeves (one for each side)

____ Lock nut and threaded tie rod

_____ **4.** Perform the necessary front wheel toe adjustment to achieve the specified toe angle on both front wheels and total toe.

Centering the Steering Wheel

Meets NATEF Task: (A4-D-8) Center Steering Wheel (P-1)

Name ________________________________ **Date** ______________________

Make/Model ___________________________ **Year** ________ **Instructor's OK** ☐

_____ **1.** Check the service information for the specified method for centering the steering wheel.

____ Remove the steering wheel and reinstall.

____ Adjust the tie rods to straighten the steering wheel and maintain proper toe adjustment.

_____ **2.** Check the service information for the specified tolerance for centering the steering wheel. Most vehicle manufacturers recommend that the spoke angle be straight within ± 3°.

Specified tolerance = _____________

_____ **3.** Test drive the vehicle and mark the steering wheel or column with masking tape when the recommended vehicle is traveling straight on a straight, level road. How much out of align is the steering wheel?

____

_____ **4.** Following the alignment equipment manufacturer's recommended procedure, adjust the tie rods until the steering wheel is straight and the front toe is still within factory specifications.

Four-Wheel Alignment

Meets NATEF Tasks: (A4-D-1 through 14) Check Alignment Angle and Perform Necessary Actions (P-1s)

Name ______________________ **Date** ______________________

Make/Model ______________________ **Year** ________ **Instructor's OK** ☐

Specifications:

	Left		Right
Camber	________		________
Caster	________		________
Toe (Total)		________	
KPI/SAI		________	
Rear Camber	________		________
Rear Toe	________		________
Rear Toe (Total)		________	

Methods of Adjustment:

	Front	Rear
Camber	______________	______________
Caster	______________	
Toe	______________	______________

Reading Before Alignment: (Record here and attach the print out.)

	Left		Right
Camber	________		________
Caster	________		________
Toe (Total)		________	
KPI/SAI		________	
Rear Camber	________		________
Rear Toe		________	
Thrust		________	
Set Back		________	

Reading After Alignment: (Record here and attach the print out.)

	Left		Right
Camber	________		________
Caster	________		________
Toe (Total)		________	
KPI/SAI		________	
Rear Camber	________		________
Rear Toe		________	
Thrust		________	
Set Back		________	

Toe Out on Turns

Meets NATEF Tasks: (A4-D-9) Check Toe-Out-On Turns (Turning Radius); Determine Necessary Action (P-2)

Name ______________________________ **Date** ____________________

Make/Model ________________________ **Year** ________ **Instructor's OK** [ ]

_____ **1.** Check the service information and determine the testing procedure and specifications for toe out on turns.

A. Testing procedure ____

____

B. Specifications ____

_____ **2.** Following the alignment equipment manufacturer's recommended procedure, measure the left and right side toe-out-on-turns.

Left side = ______________

Right side = ______________

OK ____ **NOT OK** ____

_____ **3.** If the reading does not fall within the manufacturer's specifications, what action is necessary?

____

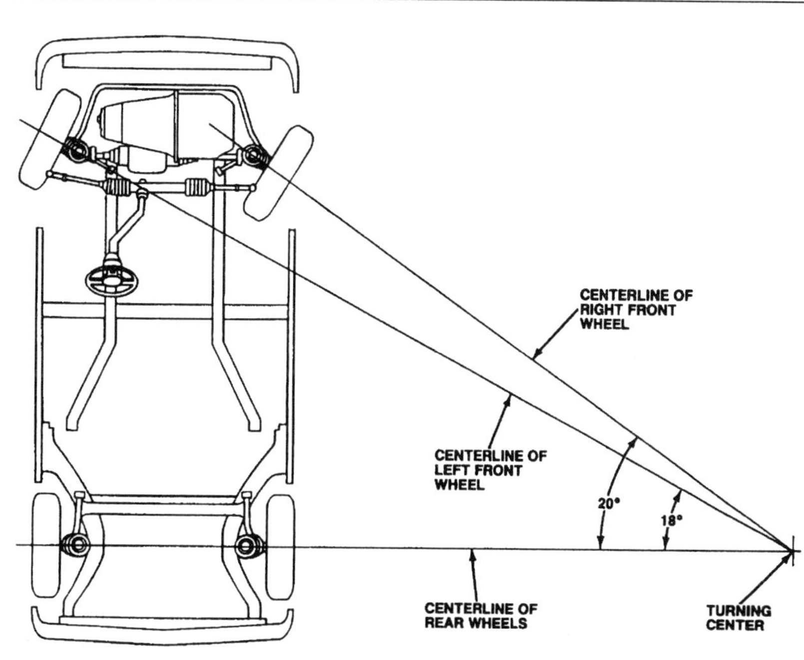

Steering Axis Inclination

Meets NATEF Tasks: (A4-D-10) Check SAI (Steering Axis Inclination) and Included Angle; Determine Necessary Action (P-2)

Name ______________________________ **Date** ____________________

Make/Model ________________________ **Year** ________ **Instructor's OK** ☐

_____ **1.** Check the service information and determine the specifications for SAI and included angle.

SAI = ________
Included angle = ________

0°
INCLUDED ANGLE
CAMBER
STEERING AXIS INCLINATION

_____ **2.** Following the alignment equipment manufacturer's recommended procedure, measure the SAI and included angles.

Left SAI = ________
Right SAI = ________
Left included angle = ________
Right included angle = ________
OK ____ **NOT OK** ____

_____ **3.** Check the service information or the chart and determine necessary action if the SAI and/or included angle are not within factory specifications.

DIAGNOSING SAI, CAMBER, AND INCLUDED ANGLE

SLA AND STRUT/SLA SUSPENSIONS

SAI	CAMBER	INCLUDED ANGLE	DIAGNOSIS
CORRECT	LESS THAN SPECS	LESS THAN SPECS OR SPINDLE	BENT STEERING KNUCKLE
LESS THAN SPECS	GREATER THAN SPECS	CORRECT	BENT LOWER CONTROL ARM
LESS THAN SPECS	GREATER THAN SPECS	GREATER THAN SPECS	BENT LOWER CONTROL ARM AND STEERING KNUCKLE OR SPINDLE
GREATER THAN SPECS	LESS THAN SPECS	CORRECT	BENT UPPER CONTROL ARM

STRUT SUSPENSIONS

SAI	CAMBER	INCLUDED ANGLE	DIAGNOSIS
CORRECT	LESS THAN SPECS	LESS THAN SPECS	BENT SPINDLE AND/OR STRUT
CORRECT	GREATER THAN SPECS	GREATER THAN SPECS	BENT SPINDLE AND/OR STRUT
LESS THAN SPECS	GREATER THAN SPECS	CORRECT	BENT CONTROL ARM OR STRUT TOWER OUT AT TOP
LESS THAN SPECS	GREATER THAN SPECS	GREATER THAN SPECS	BENT CONTROL ARM OR STRUT TOWER OUT AT TOP, ALSO BENT SPINDLE AND/OR STRUT
LESS THAN SPECS	LESS THAN SPECS	LESS THAN SPECS	BENT CONTROL ARM OR STRUT TOWER OUT AT TOP, ALSO BENT SPINDLE AND/OR STRUT
GREATER THAN SPECS	LESS THAN SPECS	CORRECT	STRUT TOWER IN AT TOP
GREATER THAN SPECS	GREATER THAN SPECS	GREATER THAN SPECS	STRUT TOWER IN AT TOP AND BENT SPINDLE AND/OR BENT STRUT

KINGPIN TWIN I-BEAM SUSPENSION

SAI(KPI)	CAMBER	INCLUDED ANGLE	DIAGNOSIS
CORRECT	GREATER THAN SPECS	GREATER THAN SPECS	BENT SPINDLE
LESS THAN SPECS	GREATER THAN SPECS	CORRECT	BENT I-BEAM
LESS THAN SPECS	GREATER THAN SPECS	GREATER THAN SPECS	BENT I-BEAM AND SPINDLE
GREATER THAN SPECS	LESS THAN SPECS	CORRECT	BENT I-BEAM

Rear Wheel Toe

Meets NATEF Tasks: (A4-D-11) Check and Adjust Rear Wheel Toe (P-2)

Name ________________________________ **Date** ______________________

Make/Model ________________________ **Year** _______ **Instructor's OK** ☐

_____ **1.** Check the service information and determine the specifications for rear wheel toe.

Total rear wheel toe specification = _______________

Left rear wheel toe specification = _______________

Right rear wheel toe specification = _______________

_____ **2.** Follow the alignment equipment manufacturer's recommended procedure and measure the rear wheel toe.

Left rear wheel toe = _______________

Right rear wheel toe = _______________

Total rear wheel toe = _______________

OK ___ **NOT OK** ___

REAR TOE ADJUSTMENT

_____ **3.** Check the service information for the recommended rear wheel toe adjustment procedure.

____ Adjusting sleeves

____ Threaded tie rod(s)

____ Shims

____ Transverse (lateral) link adjustment

____ No factory adjustment

____ Other (describe) ____

_____ **4.** Adjust the rear wheel toe, if possible. Final toe readings:

Left rear wheel toe = ___________

Right rear wheel toe = ___________

Rear Wheel Thrust Angle

Meets NATEF Tasks: (A4-D-12) Check Rear Wheel Thrust Angle; Determine Necessary Action (P-2)

Name ______________________________ **Date** ____________________

Make/Model __________________________ **Year** ________ **Instructor's OK** ☐

_____ **1.** Check the service information and determine the specification or tolerance for the rear wheel thrust angle.

Rear wheel thrust angle specification (tolerance) = ____________

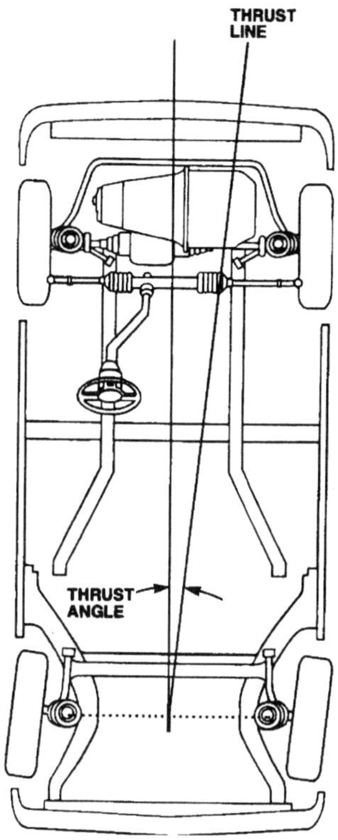

_____ **2.** Following the alignment equipment manufacturer's recommended procedure, measure the rear thrust angle.

Rear thrust angle = _________

Positive (right) ? ____

Negative (left) ? ____

_____ **3.** Check the service information and determine needed action. The difference in rear toe causes rear thrust angle, and therefore, the rear toe can often be adjusted to bring the thrust angle into specifications.

Rear toe adjustable? **Yes** ____ **No** ____

If the rear toe is not adjustable, determine what action is necessary to correct the rear thrust angle that is not within factory specifications.

____

____

Front Wheel Setback

Meets NATEF Tasks: (A4-D-13) Check for Front Wheel Setback; Determine Necessary Action (P-2)

Name ______________________________ **Date** ____________________

Make/Model ____________________________ **Year** ________ **Instructor's OK** ☐

_____ **1.** Check the service information and determine the specification or tolerance for front wheel setback.

Specification (tolerance) for front wheel setback = __________

_____ **2.** Following the alignment equipment manufacturer's recommended procedure, measure the front wheel setback.

Front wheel setback = __________

OK ____ **NOT OK** ____

_____ **3.** Consult the service information and determine the necessary action, if the front wheel setback is not within specifications.

____

____

____

____

____

____

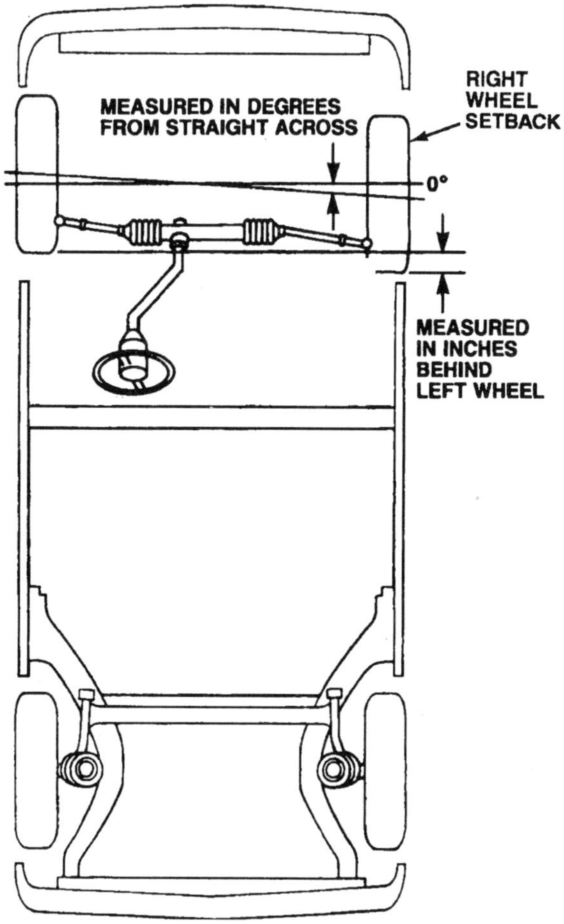

Front Cradle Alignment

Meets NATEF Tasks: (A4-D-14) Check Front Cradle (Subframe) Alignment; Determine Necessary Action (P-3)

Name ______________________________ **Date** ______________________

Make/Model ____________________________ **Year** ________ **Instructor's OK** [ ]

_____ **1.** Check the service information and determine the procedure for checking front cradle alignment.

____

____

____

_____ **2.** Following the alignment equipment manufacturer's recommended procedure, measure the left side and right side camber, included angle, and SAI.

Left camber	= ________	Right camber	= ________
Left included angle	= ________	Right included angle	= ________
Left SAI	= ________	Right SAI	= ________

Most vehicle manufacturers specify that these angles be within 0.5 degrees of each other left to right.

OK _____ **NOT OK** _____

_____ **3.** Check the service information and determine the necessary action to align the front cradle.

____

____

____

Tire Wear Patterns

Meets NATEF Tasks: (A4-E-1) Diagnose Tire Wear Patterns; Determine Necessary Action (P-1)

Name ______________________ **Date** ______________________

Make/Model ______________________ **Year** ________ **Instructor's OK** ☐

_____ **1.** Hoist the vehicle safely.

_____ **2.** Inspect all four tires for the following conditions:

A. Excessive tire wear **OK** ____ **NOT OK** ____

B. Unequal tire wear on one side (incorrect camber or toe problem) **OK** ____ **NOT OK** ____

C. Excessive wear in center of tread (overinflation) **OK** ____ **NOT OK** ____

D. Excessive wear on both outside sides (underinflation) **OK** ____ **NOT OK** ____

E. Cuts, bruises, or other physical damage (describe) ______________________ ______________________ **OK** ____ **NOT OK** ____

_____ **3.** Determine necessary action. ______________________

____

Tire Inspection and Inflation

Meets NATEF Tasks: (A4-E-2) Inspect Tires; Check and Adjust Air Pressure (P-1)

Name ______________________________ **Date** ______________________

Make/Model ________________________ **Year** ________ **Instructor's OK** ☐

_____ **1.** Check the tire information placard on the driver's door or pillar and determine the recommended air pressure.

Recommended air pressure for front tires = __________

Recommended air pressure for rear tires = __________

Recommended air pressure for spare tire = __________

_____ **2.** Check the air pressure on all of the tires and record the pressures.

Left front = ________

Right front = ________

Right rear = ________

Left rear = ________

Spare tire = ________

_____ **3.** Visually check the tires for damage or excessive wear.

OK ____ **NOT OK** ____

_____ **4.** Adjust the air pressures as needed.

Wheel/Tire Vibration Diagnosis

Meets NATEF Tasks: (A4-E-3) Diagnose Wheel/Tire Vibration, Shimmy, and Noise; Determine Necessary Action (P-2)

Name ______________________ **Date** ______________________

Make/Model ______________________ **Year** ________ **Instructor's OK** ☐

_____ **1.** Test drive the vehicle and determine the following:

Yes ___ **No** ___ Vibration is felt in steering wheel while driving.

Yes ___ **No** ___ Vibration is felt in the seat while driving.

Yes ___ **No** ___ Steering wheel shimmy is felt (back and forth motion).

Yes ___ **No** ___ Excessive tire noise is heard.

_____ **2.** Check the service information for the specified steps to reduce or eliminate vibration due to wheels or tires.

____

____

____

_____ **3.** Perform a visual inspection and check all of the tires and wheels for excessive wear or damage.

OK ___ **NOT OK** ___

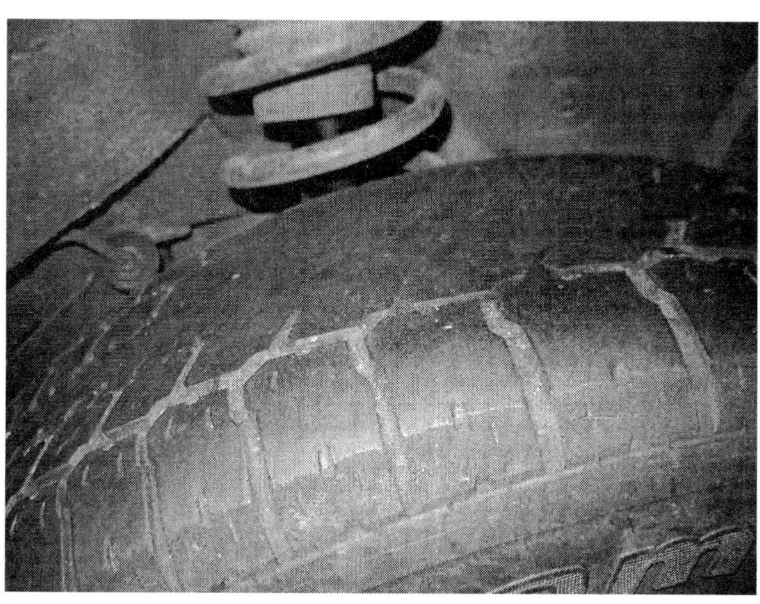

Tire Rotation

Meets NATEF Tasks: (A4-E-4) Rotate Tires According to Manufacturer's Recommendations (P-1)

Name ______________________ **Date** ______________________

Make/Model ______________________ **Year** ________ **Instructor's OK** ☐

_____ **1.** Check the service information for the recommended tire rotation method.

_____ Cannot rotate tires on this vehicle
_____ Modified X method
_____ X method
_____ Front to rear and rear to front

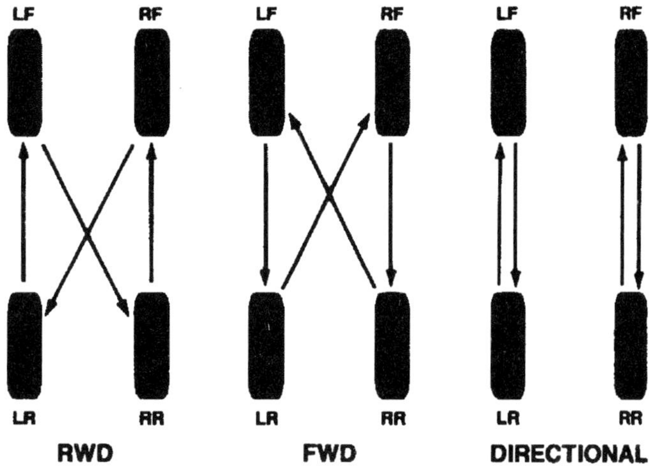

LF RF LF RF LF RF

LR RR LR RR LR RR

RWD FWD DIRECTIONAL

_____ **2.** Hoist the vehicle safely to a good working position (chest level).

_____ **3.** Remove the wheels and rotate them (if possible) according to the vehicle manufacturer's recommendation.

_____ **4.** Check and correct the tire air pressures according to the service information on the placard on the driver's door.

Specified front tire air pressure = ________

Specified rear tire air pressure = ________

_____ **5.** Lower the vehicle and move the hoist pads before driving the vehicle out of the service stall.

Tire Runout Measurement

Meets NATEF Tasks: (A4-E-5) Measure Wheel, Tire, Axle, and Hub Runout; Determine Necessary Action (P-2)

Name ______________________ **Date** ______________

Make/Model ______________________ **Year** ________ **Instructor's OK** ☐

_____ **1.** Safely hoist the vehicle until all 4 tires are approximately 2" (5 cm) off the ground.

_____ **2.** Determine the specifications for radial and lateral runout.

Specification for radial runout = _________ (usually less than 0.060 inch).

Specification for lateral runout = _________ (usually less than 0.045 inch).

_____ **3.** Using a runout gauge, rotate the tire and record the radial runout (roundness of the tires) and the lateral runout (side-to-side movement) of the tires.

HINT: Place masking tape over the tread of the tire to provide a smoother surface. This method makes it easier to read the dial indicator, especially on tires with an aggressive tread design.

Tire	Radial Runout	Lateral Runout
R.F.	______	_______
R.R.	______	_______
L.F.	______	_______
L.R.	______	_______

_____ **4.** Compare the specifications with the results.

OK ___ **NOT OK** ___

_____ **5.** Based on the measurements, what necessary action is needed?

____

____

Axle and Hub Runout Measurement

Meets NATEF Tasks: (A4-E-5) Measure Wheel, Tire, Axle, and Hub Runout; Determine Necessary Action (P-2)

Name ______________________ **Date** ______________

Make/Model ______________________ **Year** ________ **Instructor's OK** ☐

_____ **1.** Check the service information and determine the specifications for axle and hub runout.

____

_____ **2.** Hoist the vehicle safely to a good working height (chest level).

_____ **3.** Remove the wheels.

_____ **4.** Using a dial indicator, measure the axle and the hub runout.

Hub runout = ________ **OK** ____ **NOT OK** ____

Flange runout = ________ **OK** ____ **NOT OK** ____

CHECKING HUB RUNOUT

CHECKING MOUNTING FLANGE RUNOUT

_____ **5.** Check the service information and determine the necessary action. ______________

____

____

Tire Pull Diagnosis

Meets NATEF Tasks: (A4-E-6) Diagnose Tire Pull (Lead) Problems;
Determine Necessary Action (P-2)

Name ______________________________ **Date** ______________________

Make/Model ________________________ **Year** ________ **Instructor's OK** ☐

_____ **1.** Check and correct tire air pressures as per vehicle manufacturer's specifications.

_____ **2.** Visually check the tires for faults.

OK ____ **NOT OK** ____ (replace defective tires)

_____ **3.** Test drive the vehicle on a straight, level road.

_____ **4.** The vehicle pulls (leads) toward the:

_____ Right

_____ Left

_____ **5.** A pull or lead can be due to tire conicity or ply steer. To diagnose if the pull or lead is tire related, rotate the front tires to opposite sides of the vehicle.

OK ____ **NOT OK** ____

_____ **6.** If not OK, rotate the rear tires to opposite sides of the vehicle.

OK ____ **NOT OK** ____

_____ **7.** If not OK, rotate the front tires to the rear and the rear tires to the front.

OK ____ **NOT OK** ____

_____ **8.** Based on the tests performed, what action is needed? ______________________

____

____

____

Tire Balance

Meets NATEF Task: (A4-E-7) Balance Wheel and Tire Assembly (Static and Dynamic) (P-1)

Name ______________________________ **Date** ______________________

Make/Model ________________________ **Year** ________ **Instructor's OK** ☐

_____ **1.** Perform the pre-balance checks.

A. Check tire pressure.

B. Remove grease/dirt from inside of the rim.

C. Remove stones from the tread.

_____ **2.** Follow the tire balancing equipment manufacturer's procedures.

_____ **3.** Wheel width? ____________ in.

_____ **4.** Wheel diameter? ____________ in.

_____ **5.** Check balance before removing old weights.

HINT: This will help in the diagnosis of a vibration knowing that one or more wheels were not balanced.

_____ **6.** Out of balance with old or no weights:

inside = __________ outside = __________

_____ **7.** Did the tire balance OK?

OK __________ **NOT OK** __________

If not OK, explain why: ______________________________

____

____

Tire Changing

Meets NATEF Task: (A4-E-8) Dismount, Inspect, Repair, and Remount Tire on the Wheel (P-2)

Name ______________________________ **Date** ______________________

Make/Model __________________________ **Year** ________ **Instructor's OK** ☐

_____ **1.** Be sure you are wearing approved safety glasses.

_____ **2.** Slowly remove the Schrader valve using a tire valve tool and deflate the tire.

_____ **3.** Place the tire against the tire changing machine and "break the bead" front and back following the tire machine manufacturer's instructions.

_____ **4.** Secure the tire and wheel assembly onto the machine.

_____ **5.** Remove the tire from the rim using the proper procedure.

_____ **6.** Install the replacement tire on the rim using the proper procedure.

_____ **7.** Inflate and seat the tire beads using the procedure.

CAUTION: Do not exceed 40 psi air pressure to seat the tire bead.

_____ **8.** Install the valve core and check for leaks.

_____ **9.** Inflate the tires to vehicle specifications.

Torque Wheel Lug Nuts

Meets NATEF Task: (A4-E-9) Reinstall Wheel; Torque Lug Nuts (P-1)

Name ________________________________ **Date** ______________________

Make/Model ___________________________ **Year** ________ **Instructor's OK** ☐

_____ **1.** Determine the vehicle manufacturer's specified lug nut torque specification.

__________ (usually between 80 and 100 lb-ft)

_____ **2.** Use a hand-operated wire brush on the wheel studs to ensure clean and dry threads and check for damage.

OK _____ **NOT OK** _____ Describe fault: ______________________

_____ **3.** Verify that the lug nuts are OK and free of defects.

CAUTION: Some vehicle manufacturers warn to not lubricate the wheel studs because this can cause the lug nuts to loosen while the vehicle is being driven, resulting in personal injury.

_____ **4.** Install the wheel over the studs and start all lug nuts (or bolts) by hand.

_____ **5.** Tighten the lug nuts a little at a time in a star pattern using an air impact wrench equipped with the proper torque limiting adapter or a torque wrench.

_____ Used a torque wrench

_____ Used an air impact with a torque limiting adapter

_____ **6.** Tighten the lug nuts to final torque in a star pattern.

NOTE: "Tighten one, skip one, tighten one" is the usual method if four or five lug nuts are used.

Tire Repair

Meets NATEF Task: (A4-E-10) Inspect and Repair Tire (P-2)

Name ______________________ **Date** ______________________

Make/Model ______________________ **Year** ________ **Instructor's OK** ☐

_____ **1.** Locate the source of the leak by submerging the tire under water or by spraying the tire with soapy water. Describe the location of the leak.

____

_____ **2.** Remove the foreign object and use a reamer to clean the hole in the tire (tread area only).

_____ **3.** Dismount the tire and buff the inside of the tire around the hole.

_____ **4.** Apply rubber cement to the buffed area.

_____ **5.** Insert the repair plug from the inside of the tire.

_____ **6.** Pull the plug through the puncture from the outside of the tire.

_____ **7.** Use a stitching tool to make sure the inside of the patch is well adhered to the inside of the tire.

_____ **8.** Remove the tire and inflate to the air pressure specified by the vehicle manufacturer.

_____ **9.** Check the repair for air leaks using soapy water.

OK ____ **NOT OK** ____

Appendix 1

Brakes (A5)

NATEF Task List and Correlation Chart

Brakes (A5)

NATEF TASK LIST

NATEF Task List	Page #	Date Completed	Instructor's OK
A. General Brake Systems Diagnosis **P-1:**			
1. Identify and interpret brake system concerns; determine necessary action.	8		
2. Research applicable vehicle and service information, such as brake system operation, vehicle service history, service precautions, and technical service bulletins.	6, 7		
3. Locate and interpret vehicle and major component identification numbers (VIN, vehicle certification labels, calibration decals).	5		
B. Hydraulic System Diagnosis and Repair **P-1**			
1. Diagnose pressure concerns in the brake system using hydraulic principles (Pascal's Law).	13		
2. Remove, bench bleed, and reinstall master cylinder.	11		
3. Diagnose poor stopping, pulling or dragging concerns caused by malfunctions in the hydraulic system; determine necessary action.	14		
4. Select, handle, store, and fill brake fluids to proper level.	17		
5. Bleed (manual, pressure, vacuum or surge) brake system.	22, 23, 24, 25, 26		

NATEF Task List	Page #	Date Completed	Instructor's OK
B. Hydraulic System Diagnosis and Repair **P-2:**			
1. Measure brake pedal height; determine necessary action.	10		
2. Check master cylinder for internal and external leaks and proper operation; determine necessary action.	12		
3. Inspect brake lines, flexible hoses, and fittings for leaks, dents, kinks, rust, cracks, bulging or wear; tighten loose fittings and supports; determine necessary action.	15		
4. Fabricate and/or install brake lines (double flare and ISO types); replace hoses, fittings, and supports as needed.	16		
5. Inspect, test, and/or replace metering (hold-off), proportioning (balance), pressure differential, and combination valves.	18, 19, 20		
B. Hydraulic System Diagnosis and Repair **P-3**			
1. Inspect, test, and adjust height (load) sensing proportioning valve.	21		
2. Inspect, test, and/or replace components of brake warning light system.	9		
3. Flush hydraulic system.	27		
C. Drum Brake Diagnosis and Repair **P-1:**			
1. Diagnose poor stopping, noise, pulling, grabbing, dragging or pedal pulsation concerns; determine necessary action.	28		

NATEF Task List	Page #	Date Completed	Instructor's OK
2. Remove, clean (using proper safety procedures), inspect, and measure brake drums; service or replace as needed.	29		
3. Refinish brake drum.	30		
4. Remove, clean, and inspect brake shoes, springs, pins, clips, levers, adjusters/self-adjusters, other related brake hardware, and backing support plates; lubricate and reassemble.	31, 32, 33, 34		
5. Pre-adjust brake shoes and parking brake before installing brake drums or drum/hub assemblies and wheel bearings.	36		
6. Install wheel, torque lug nuts, and make final checks and adjustments.	37		
C. Drum Brake Diagnosis and Repair P-2:			
1. Remove, inspect, and install wheel cylinders.	35		
D. Disc Brake Diagnosis and Repair P-1:			
1. Diagnose poor stopping, noise, pulling, grabbing, dragging or pedal pulsation concerns; determine necessary action.	38		
2. Remove caliper assembly from mountings; clean and inspect for leaks and damage to caliper housing; determine necessary action.	39, 41		
3. Clean and inspect caliper mounting and slides for wear and damage; determine necessary action.	38		
4. Remove, clean, and inspect pads and retaining hardware; determine necessary action.	40		

NATEF Task List	Page #	Date Completed	Instructor's OK
5. Reassemble, lubricate, and reinstall caliper, pads, and related hardware; seat pads, and inspect for leaks.	40		
6. Clean, inspect, and measure rotor with a dial indicator and a micrometer; follow manufacturer's recommendations in determining need to machine or replace.	43		
7. Remove and reinstall rotor.	44		
8. Refinish rotor according to manufacturer's recommendations.	45, 46		
9. Install wheel, torque lug nuts, and make final checks and adjustments.	37		
D. Disc Brake Diagnosis and Repair P-2:			
1. Disassemble and clean caliper assembly; inspect parts for wear, rust, scoring, and damage; replace seal, boot, and damaged or worn parts.	42		
D. Disc Brake Diagnosis and Repair P-3:			
1. Adjust calipers with integrated parking brake system.	47		
E. Power Assist Units Diagnosis and Repair P-2:			
1. Test pedal free travel with and without engine running; check power assist operation.	48		
2. Check vacuum supply (manifold or auxiliary pump) to vacuum-type power booster.	48		
3. Inspect the vacuum-type power booster unit for vacuum leaks; inspect the check valve for proper operation; determine necessary action.	48		

NATEF Task List	Page #	Date Completed	Instructor's OK
E. Power Assist Units Diagnosis and Repair P-3:			
1. Inspect and test hydro-boost system and accumulator for leaks and proper operation; determine necessary action.	49		
F. Miscellaneous (Wheel Bearings, Parking Brakes, Electrical, Etc.) Diagnosis and Repair P-1:			
1. Diagnose wheel bearing noises, wheel shimmy, and vibration concerns; determine necessary action.	50		
2. Remove, clean, inspect, repack, and install wheel bearings and replace seals; install hub and adjust wheel bearings.	51,		
3. Check parking brake operation; adjust as needed.	53		
4. Check operation of brake stop light system; adjust and service as needed.	54		
5. Replace wheel bearing and race.	55		
6. Inspect and replace wheel studs.	56		
F. Miscellaneous (Wheel Bearings, Parking Brakes, Electrical, Etc.) Diagnosis and Repair P-2:			
1. Check parking brake cables and components for wear, rusting, binding, and corrosion; clean, lubricate, and replace as needed.	53		
2. Remove and reinstall sealed wheel bearing assembly.	52		

NATEF Task List	Page #	Date Completed	Instructor's OK
F. Miscellaneous (Wheel Bearings, Parking Brakes, Electrical, Etc.) Diagnosis and Repair P-3:			
1. Check operation of parking brake indicator light system.	9		
G. Anti-lock Brake System P-1:			
1. Identify and inspect antilock brake system (ABS) components; determine necessary action.	57, 59		
2. Diagnose anti-lock brake system (ABS) electronic control(s) and components using self-diagnosis and/or recommended test equipment; determine necessary action.	60		
3. Test, diagnose and service ABS speed sensors, toothed ring (tone wheel), and circuits using a graphing multimeter (GMM)/digital storage oscilloscope (DSO) (includes output signal, resistance, shorts to voltage/ground, and frequency data).	62		
G. Anti-lock Brake System P-2:			
1. Diagnose poor stopping, wheel lock-up, abnormal pedal feel or pulsation, and noise concerns caused by the anti-lock brake system (ABS); determine necessary action.	58		
2. Bleed the anti-lock brake system's (ABS) front and rear hydraulic circuits.	64		

NATEF Task List	Page #	Date Completed	Instructor's OK
G. Anti-lock Brake System **P-3:**			
1. Depressurize high-pressure components of the anti-lock brake system (ABS).	63		
2. Remove and install antilock brake system (ABS) electrical/electronic and hydraulic components.	65		
3. Diagnose antilock brake system (ABS) braking concerns caused by vehicle modifications (tire size, curb height, final drive ratio, etc.).	66		
4. Identify traction control system components.	57		

Appendix 2

Suspension and Steering (A4)

NATEF Task List and Correlation Chart

Suspension and Steering (A4)

NATEF TASK LIST

NATEF Task List	Page #	Date Completed	Instructor's OK
A. General Suspension and Steering Systems Diagnosis P-1:			
1. Identify and interpret suspension and steering concern; determine necessary action.	67 68 69 90 92		
2. Research applicable vehicle and service information, such as suspension and steering system operation, vehicle service history, service precautions, and technical service bulletins.	5, 69		
3. Locate and interpret vehicle and major component identification numbers (VIN, vehicle certification labels, calibration decals).	5, 69		
B. Steering Systems Diagnosis and Repair P-1:			
1. Disable and enable supplemental restraint system (SRS).	70		
2. Remove and replace steering wheel; center/time supplemental restraint system (SRS) coil (clock spring).	71		
3. Remove and replace manual or power rack and pinion steering gear; inspect mounting bushings and brackets.	78		
4. Inspect and replace manual or power rack and pinion steering gear inner tie rod ends (sockets) and bellows boots.	79		
5. Inspect power steering fluid levels and condition.	80		
6. Remove, inspect, replace, and adjust power steering pump belt.	83		
7. Inspect, replace, and adjust tie rod ends (sockets), tie rod sleeves, and clamps.	88		
B. Steering Systems Diagnosis and Repair P-2:			
1. Diagnose steering column noises, looseness, and binding concerns (including tilt mechanisms); determine necessary action.	72		

NATEF Task List	Page #	Date Completed	Instructor's OK
2. Inspect steering shaft universal-joint(s), flexible coupling(s), collapsible column, lock cylinder mechanism, and steering wheel; perform necessary action.	76		
3. Flush, fill, and bleed power steering system.	81		
4. Diagnose power steering fluid leakage; determine necessary action.	82		
5. Inspect and replace power steering hoses and fittings.	86		
6. Inspect and replace pitman arm, relay (centerlink/intermediate) rod, idler arm and mountings, and steering linkage damper.	87		
B. Steering Systems Diagnosis and Repair P-3:			
1. Diagnose power steering gear (non-rack and pinion) binding, uneven turning effort, looseness, hard steering, and fluid leakage concerns; determine necessary action.	73		
2. Diagnose power steering gear (rack and pinion) binding, uneven turning effort, looseness, hard steering, and fluid leakage concerns; determine necessary action.	75		
3. Adjust manual or power non-rack and pinion worm bearing preload and sector lash.	77		
4. Remove and reinstall power steering pump.	84		
5. Remove and reinstall power steering pump pulley; check pulley and belt alignment.	85		
6. Test and diagnose components of electronically controlled steering systems using a scan tool; determine necessary action.	89		
C. Suspension Systems Diagnosis and Repair 1. Front Suspensions P-1:			
1. Diagnose short and long arm suspension system noises body sway and uneven riding height concerns; determine necessary action.	90		
2. Diagnose strut suspension system noises body sway and uneven riding height concerns; determine necessary action.	91		
3. Remove, inspect, and install strut cartridge or assembly strut coil spring insulators (silencers) and upper strut bearing mount.	102		

NATEF Task List	Page #	Date Completed	Instructor's OK
C. Suspension Systems Diagnosis and Repair **1. Front Suspensions** **P-2:**			
1. Remove, inspect, and install strut rods (compression/tension) and bushings.	94		
2. Remove, inspect, and install upper and lower ball-joints.	95, 96		
3. Remove, inspect, and install steering knuckle assemblies.	97 98		
4. Remove, inspect, and install short and long arm suspension system coil springs and spring insulators.	90, 99		
5. Remove, inspect, and install stabilizer bar bushings, brackets, and links.	101		
6. Lubricate suspension and steering systems.	103		
C. Suspension Systems Diagnosis and Repair **1. Front Suspensions** **P-3:**			
1. Remove, inspect, and install upper and lower control arms, bushings, shafts, and rebound bumpers.	93		
2. Remove, inspect, install and adjust suspension system torsion bars; inspect mounts.	99		
C. Suspension Systems Diagnosis and Repair **2. Rear Suspensions** **P-2:**			
1. Remove, inspect, and install coil springs and spring insulators.	104		
2. Remove, inspect, and install transverse links, control arms, bushings, and mounts.	105		
3. Remove, inspect, and install strut cartridge or assembly strut coil spring and insulators (silencers).	107		
C. Suspension Systems Diagnosis and Repair **2. Rear Suspensions** **P-3:**			
1. Remove, inspect, and install leaf springs, leaf spring insulators (silencers), shackles, brackets, bushings, and mounts.	106		
C. Suspension Systems Diagnosis and Repair **3. Miscellaneous Service** **P-1:**			
1. Inspect, remove, and replace shock absorbers.	108, 109		

NATEF Task List	Page #	Date Completed	Instructor's OK
2. Remove, inspect, and service or replace front and rear wheel bearings.	110		
C. Suspension Systems Diagnosis and Repair 3. Miscellaneous Service P-3:			
1. Test and diagnose components of electronically controlled suspension systems using a scan tool; determine necessary action.	111		
D. Wheel Alignment Diagnosis, Adjustment, and Repair P-1:			
1. Differentiate between steering and suspension concerns using principles of steering geometry (caster, camber, toe, etc.).	112		
2. Diagnose vehicle wander, drift, pull, hard steering, bump steer, memory steer, torque steer, and steering return concerns; determine necessary action.	113		
3. Perform prealignment inspection; perform necessary action.	114, 115, 116		
4. Measure vehicle ride height; determine necessary action.	117		
5. Check and adjust front and rear wheel camber; perform necessary action.	118, 122		
6. Check and adjust caster; perform necessary action.	119, 122		
7. Check and adjust front wheel toe; adjust as needed.	120, 122		
8. Center steering wheel.	121, 122		
D. Wheel Alignment Diagnosis, Adjustment, and Repair P-2:			
1. Check toe-out-on-turns (turning radius); determine necessary action.	123		
2. Check SAI (steering axis inclination) and included angle; determine necessary action.	124		
3. Check and adjust rear wheel toe.	125		
4. Check rear wheel thrust angle; determine necessary action.	126		
5. Check for front wheel setback; determine necessary action.	127		
D. Wheel Alignment Diagnosis, Adjustment, and Repair P-3:			
1. Check front cradle (subframe) alignment; determine necessary action.	128		

NATEF Task List	Page #	Date Completed	Instructor's OK
E. Wheel and Tire Diagnosis and Repair P-1:			
1. Diagnose tire wear patterns; determine necessary action.	129		
2. Inspect tires; check and adjust air pressure.	130		
3. Rotate tires according to manufacturer's recommendations.	132		
4. Balance wheel and tire assembly (static and dynamic).	136		
5. Reinstall wheel; torque lug nuts.	138		
E. Wheel and Tire Diagnosis and Repair P-2:			
1. Diagnose wheel/tire vibration, shimmy, and noise concerns; determine necessary action.	131		
2. Measure wheel, tire, axle, and hub runout; determine necessary action.	133, 134		
3. Diagnose tire pull (lead) concern; determine necessary action.	135		
4. Dismount, inspect, repair, and remount tire on wheel.	137		
5. Inspect and repair tire.	139